The MAILBOX®

The Education Center®

Math Practice Pages

grade 5

S0-AZQ-806

Over **80** engaging reproducibles for building **number and operations skills!**

- Number Sense

- Addition and Subtraction

- Multiplication

- Division

- Fractions

- Decimals

Use to reteach, reinforce, and assess!

Managing Editor: Peggy Hambright

Editorial Team: Becky S. Andrews, Diane Badden, Kimberley Bruck, Karen A. Brudnak, Kitty Campbell, Chris Curry, Lynette Dickerson, Theresa Lewis Goode, Tazmen Hansen, Marsha Heim, Lori Z. Henry, Debra Liverman, Dorothy C. McKinney, Thad H. McLaurin, Sharon Murphy, Jennifer Nunn, Amy Payne, Mark Rainey, Hope Rodgers, Eliseo De Jesus Santos II, Becky Saunders, Barry Slate, Zane Williard

www.themailbox.com

©2008 The Mailbox® Books
All rights reserved.
ISBN10 #1-56234-797-7 • ISBN13 #978-156234-797-0

Manufactured in the United States
10 9 8 7 6 5 4 3 2 1

Table of Contents

Number Sense

Basic Operations

Addition and Subtraction

Multiplication Basics

Multiplying With No Regrouping

Multiplying With One Regrouping

Multiplying With More Than One Regrouping

Division Basics

Dividing by One Digit

Dividing by Two Digits

Fractions

Fraction Basics

Adding and Subtracting Fractions

Multiplying Fractions

Decimals

Decimal Basics

Adding and Subtracting Decimals

Multiplying Decimals

Dividing Decimals

Answer Keys

Name _____ Date _____

Burger Builder

Glue the missing part(s) to each burger.

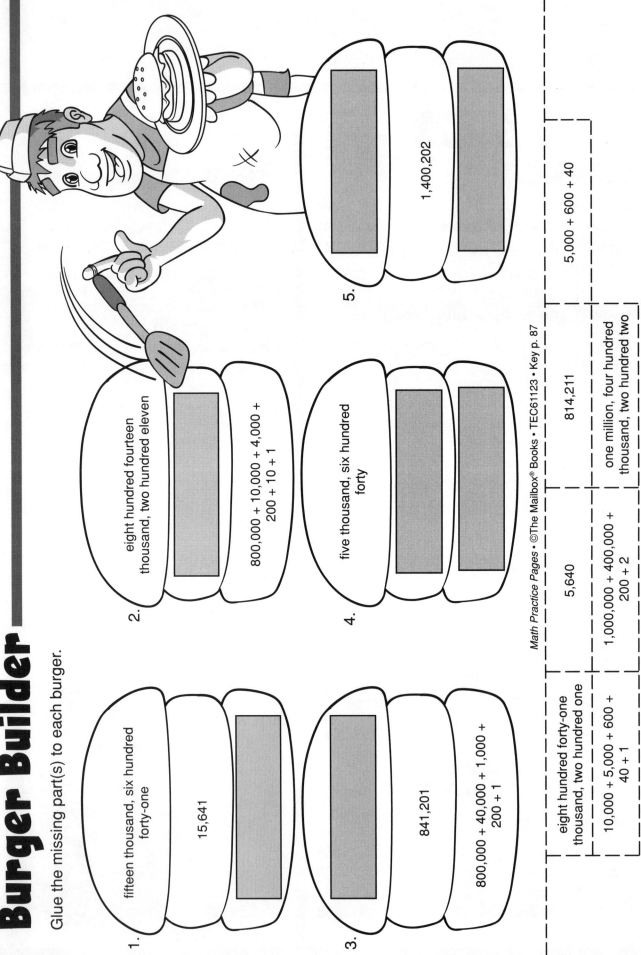

1. fifteen thousand, six hundred forty-one

   15,641

2. eight hundred fourteen thousand, two hundred eleven

   800,000 + 10,000 + 4,000 + 200 + 10 + 1

3. 841,201

   800,000 + 40,000 + 1,000 + 200 + 1

4. five thousand, six hundred forty

5. 1,400,202

Math Practice Pages • ©The Mailbox® Books • TEC61123 • Key p. 87

| eight hundred forty-one thousand, two hundred one | 5,640 | 814,211 | 5,000 + 600 + 40 |
| 10,000 + 5,000 + 600 + 40 + 1 | 1,000,000 + 400,000 + 200 + 2 | one million, four hundred thousand, two hundred two | |

Number sense: number forms

Name _____ Date _____

Catch the Crook!

Lightly shade the box that tells whether the place value listed for the underlined digit is correct or incorrect.

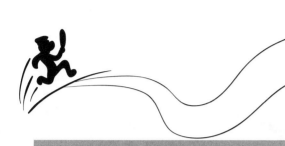

	Number	Place Value	Correct	Incorrect
1.	8,2̲64,795	hundreds	O	L
2.	9̲,530,678	millions	M	F
3.	1,6̲45,981	millions	E	Y
4.	2,1̲20	tens	L	P
5.	2̲,563,400	millions	U	M
6.	99̲9,000	hundred thousands	S	E
7.	1,798,64̲2	ones	W	T
8.	6,2̲79	thousands	R	N
9.	8̲9,463	ten thousands	B	E
10.	798,4̲07	hundreds	C	E
11.	8,041̲,367	millions	T	D
12.	3,6̲40,109	hundred thousands	F	A
13.	8,6̲45	tens	N	G
14.	7̲,616,450	millions	K	D
15.	93̲1,648	hundred thousands	V	L
16.	45̲6,789	thousands	I	H
17.	316,98̲2	tens	S	N
18.	1̲0,498	ten thousands	T	E

Write in order the letters of the unshaded boxes to reveal where the crook was caught.

The crook was caught at the corner _____.

Fill Out the Tag

Round each number to each nearest place listed.

1. 1,887,654

ten = _____

hundred = _____

thousand = _____

ten thousand = _____

hundred thousand = _____

million = _____

2. 3,406,792

ten = _____

hundred = _____

thousand = _____

ten thousand = _____

hundred thousand = _____

million = _____

3. 5,056,135

ten = _____

hundred = _____

thousand = _____

ten thousand = _____

hundred thousand = _____

million = _____

4. 8,107,453

ten = _____

hundred = _____

thousand = _____

ten thousand = _____

hundred thousand = _____

million = _____

5. 4,610,047

ten = _____

hundred = _____

thousand = _____

ten thousand = _____

hundred thousand = _____

million = _____

6. 2,864,209

ten = _____

hundred = _____

thousand = _____

ten thousand = _____

hundred thousand = _____

million = _____

Getting New Shoes

Write < or > in each horseshoe.

1. 120,053  142,800

2. 46,927  43,692

3. 1,103,298  1,104,298

4. 5,264  998

5. 1,208  1,002

6. 6,965,079 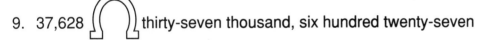 6,965,097

7. 24,907  249,007

8. 378  3,780

9. 37,628 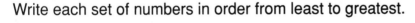 thirty-seven thousand, six hundred twenty-seven

10. 18 thousand ___ 18,020

Write each set of numbers in order from least to greatest.

11. 301; 3,010; 3,001; 3,100; 3,030,001 _____

_____

12. 10,011; 1,011; 10,010; 1,101; 10,001 _____

_____

13. 325; 2,620; 2,358; 906 _____

14. 286; 590; 18,137; 5,590 _____

15. 679; 662,720; 6,738; 660,984 _____

Name _____ Date _____

Movie Snack

Add.

1.   368
   + 275

2.   1,499
   + 108

3.   937
   + 43

4. 51,238
   + 1,698

5.   2,606
   + 1,474

6.   1,798
   +   46

7.   4,080
   + 6,578

8.   586
   + 414

9.   427
   + 182

10.   879
    + 320

11.   2,419
    + 3,081

12. 15,075
    + 6,025

Number Whiz

Add.

1. 1,420
    336
    + 219
    _____ = O

2. 216
    3,751
    + 6,032
    _____ = A

3. 4,895
    16,387
    + 723,198
    _____ = C

4. 9,703
    192
    + 805
    _____ = U

5. 51,264
    1,075
    + 698
    _____ = N

6. 375
    304
    + 1,826
    _____ = A

7. 125
    4,674
    + 5,201
    _____ = N

8. 8,602
    125
    + 707
    _____ = C

9. 1,745
    3,929
    + 6,217
    _____ = T

10. 3,692
    15,071
    + 345,927
    _____ = T

1,878; 1,879; 1,880...

What kind of ant is good at counting?
To find out, write each letter from above on its matching numbered line below.

an ___ ___ ___ ___ ___ ___ ___ ___ ___ ___
   2,505 744,480 9,434 1,975 10,700 10,000 364,690 9,999 53,037 11,891

Time to Unload

Subtract.

① 2,670
− 896

② 6,030
− 3,251

③ 409
− 220

④ 69,005
− 12,972

⑤ 6,025
− 2,150

⑥ 200,100
− 124,809

⑦ 5,001
− 2,312

⑧ 800,000
− 612,935

⑨ 3,075
− 839

⑩ 900,000
− 411,132

Name _____ Date _____

The Great Outdoors

Add or subtract.

1. Greg climbed a hiking trail that began at 3,075 feet. The trail ended at 4,140 feet. How many feet did Greg climb?

   _____ feet

2. Jenny's hiking club climbed 2,085 feet above sea level. The hikers started their climb from a point at 729 feet above sea level. How many feet did the club members climb?

   _____ feet

3. Will and his friends climbed to the top of a mountain that was 4,003 feet above sea level. They started their climb at 1,895 feet. How many feet did they climb?

   _____ feet

4. Erin and her family walked 12,806 steps on one trail. They walked 11,076 steps on a second trail. How many steps did she and her family walk in all?

   _____ steps

5. Colin biked across one bridge that was 1,379 meters long. He biked across another bridge that was 2,088 meters long. How much longer was the second bridge?

   _____ meters

6. A national park manager rented cabins to 10,829 hikers one month and 20,028 hikers the next month. How many more hikers rented cabins the second month than the first?

   _____ hikers

7. Amber and her friends kayaked 8,800 yards on a river one day and 12,320 yards the next. They kayaked 10,550 yards the last day. How many yards did she and her friends kayak in all?

   _____ yards

8. Campers spent $4,079.34 at a snack store one day and $3,095.62 the next. How much more did campers spend the first day than the second?

   _____ more

Name _____   Date _____

Tasty Treats

Write the letter of the best estimate.

1. 5,650 + 882 + 959 + 273 = _____
    A. 5,000   B. 7,000   C. 8,000   D. 6,000

2. 6,365 − 876 = _____
    A. 6,000   B. 5,000   C. 7,000   D. 4,000

3. 9,298 − 2,307 = _____
    A. 7,000   B. 9,000   C. 6,000   D. 8,000

4. 8,241 + 754 + 109 = _____
    A. 12, 000   B. 9,000   C. 8,000   D. 7,000

5. $18.37 − $7.98 = _____
    A. $13.00   B. $18.00   C. $15.00   D. $10.00

6. 3,406 + 2,679 = _____
    A. 6,000   B. 5,000   C. 4,000   D. 3,000

7. 5,346 − 289 = _____
    A. 3,000   B. 2,000   C. 5,000   D. 4,000

8. 12,090 + 32,665 + 28,769 = _____
    A. 70,000   B. 60,000   C. 80,000   D. 50,000

9. 52,325 − 8,912 = _____
    A. < 33,000   B. < 30,000   C. > 44,000   D. > 40,000

10. 398 + 456 + 767 = _____
    A. > 1,700   B. > 2,000   C. < 1,700   D. < 1,400

Brushing Up on Facts

Multiply.

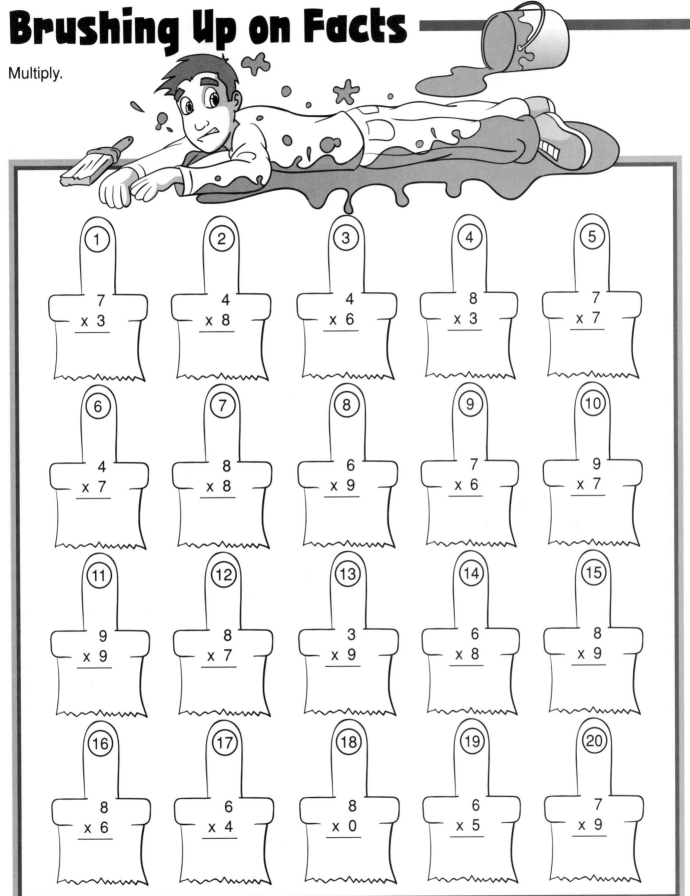

1. 7
   x 3

2. 4
   x 8

3. 4
   x 6

4. 8
   x 3

5. 7
   x 7

6. 4
   x 7

7. 8
   x 8

8. 6
   x 9

9. 7
   x 6

10. 9
   x 7

11. 9
   x 9

12. 8
   x 7

13. 3
   x 9

14. 6
   x 8

15. 8
   x 9

16. 8
   x 6

17. 6
   x 4

18. 8
   x 0

19. 6
   x 5

20. 7
   x 9

Trip's Triple-Decker Sandwich

Round to the greatest place value.
Then estimate the product.

1. 612
   x 7
   T

2. 909
   x 5
   O

3. 471
   x 7
   S

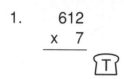

4. 368
   x 8
   U

5. $2.78
   x 9
   C

6. 328
   x 6
   L

7. 607
   x 4
   A

8. 519
   x 8
   C

9. $8.25
   x 9
   A

10. 5,174
    x 5
    P

11. 4,199
    x 4
    I

12. $15.35
    x 6
    D

13. 6,541
    x 7
    E

14. 6,419
    x 8
    L

15. 9,034
    x 7
    C

To learn the name of Trip's favorite sandwich, write each letter from above on its matching numbered line below.

```
___  ___  ___  ___  ___ - ___  ___  ___
$72.00  4,000  4,500  1,800  $120.00  $27.00  3,200  4,200
```

```
___  ___  ___  ___  ___  ___  ___
3,500  25,000  49,000  63,000  16,000  2,400  48,000
```

Secret Code

Round each factor to the greatest place value.
Write the estimated product.
Then cross out the matching number code in the box.

1.   48
   x 34

2.   28
   x 37

3.   45
   x 77

4.   37
   x 53

5.   39
   x 24

6.   61
   x 52

7.   94
   x 36

8.   26
   x 72

9.   59
   x 29

10.   98
   x 83

11.   75
   x 65

12.   44
   x 79

Codes
4-0-0-0
3-6-0-0
8-0-0-0
1-8-0-0
6-2-0-0
3-2-0-0
2-0-0-0
1-5-0-0
8-0-0
5-6-0-0
3-0-0-0
2-1-0-0
1-2-0-0

The number that is not crossed out is the access code.

The code is _____.

Time for Tires

Glue each tire to its matching car and estimation method.

1.
364
x 219

R   F-E

2.
428
x 656

R   F-E

3.
817
x 225

R   F-E

4.
769
x 503

R   F-E

5.
248
x 876

R   F-E

6.
642
x 357

R   F-E

R means round to the greatest place value. *F-E* means use front-end estimation.

Math Practice Pages • ©The Mailbox® Books • TEC61123 • Key p. 88

240,000   400,000   160,000   80,000   180,000   280,000

160,000   60,000   240,000   180,000   160,000   350,000

16 Multiplication: estimating products

Name _____ Date _____

All Kinds of Cycles

Round each factor to the greatest place value. Then estimate the product.

1. _____
   unicycles

3. _____
   bicycles built
   for two

5. _____
   scooters

7. _____
   motorcycles

1. A unicycle factory makes 435 unicycles each day for 315 days. About how many unicycles does the factory produce?

2. A bicycle factory makes 529 mountain bikes each day for 278 days. About how many mountain bikes does the factory produce?

3. A different bicycle factory makes 136 bicycles built for two each day for 195 days. About how many bicycles built for two does the factory produce?

4. A tricycle factory makes 787 tricycles each day for 341 days. About how many tricycles does the factory produce?

5. A scooter factory makes 374 scooters each day for 358 days. About how many scooters does the factory produce?

6. A moped factory makes 217 mopeds each day for 198 days. About how many mopeds does the factory produce?

7. A motorcycle factory makes 158 motorcycles each day for 322 days. About how many motorcycles does the factory produce?

8. A scooter factory sells 916 electric scooters for $107 each. About how much money does the factory receive for these scooters?

2. _____
   mountain
   bikes

4. _____
   tricycles

6. _____
   mopeds

8. _____
   electric scooters

Race to the Finish

Multiply.

To show the path to the finish line, connect the boxes with products less than 5,000.

Start

1. 3,343
   x   2
   ☐

2. 2,120
   x   3
   ☐

3. 231
   x   3
   ☐

4. 4,431
   x   2
   ☐

5. 3,421
   x   2
   ☐

6. 2,342
   x   2
   ☐

7. 303
   x   3
   ☐

8. 1,033
   x   3
   ☐

9. 3,432
   x   2
   ☐

10. 2,123
    x   3
   ☐

11. 404
    x   2
   ☐

12. 431
    x   2
   ☐

13. 210
    x   3
   ☐

14. 2,021
    x   4
   ☐

15. 3,131
    x   3
   ☐

16. 4,321
    x   2
   ☐

17. 4,234
    x   2
   ☐

18. 3,441
    x   2
   ☐

19. 1,012
    x   4
   ☐

20. 3,012
    x   3
   ☐

FINISH

Name _____   Date _____

Dragon Trainers

Multiply.

(1)　34
　　x 21

(2)　14
　　x 12

(3)　41
　　x 12

(4)　42
　　x 20

(5)　29
　　x 11

☐ = S　　☐ = G　　☐ = E　　☐ = I　　☐ = W

(6)　37
　　x 11

(7)　31
　　x 23

(8)　13
　　x 13

(9)　217
　　x 11

(10)　121
　　x 14

☐ = A　　☐ = R　　☐ = S　　☐ = N　　☐ = E

(11)　334
　　x 20

(12)　224
　　x 12

(13)　519
　　x 11

(14)　433
　　x 22

(15)　8,787
　　x　 11

☐ = I　　☐ = D　　☐ = R　　☐ = V　　☐ = I

(16)　9,813
　　x　 11

(17)　4,341
　　x 21

(18)　1,344
　　x 21

☐ = A　　☐ = B　　☐ = E

(19)　3,031
　　x　 13

(20)　3,123
　　x　 23

☐ = I　　☐ = R

To find out which knights are training the dragon, write each letter from above on its matching numbered line below.

____ ____ ____ 　 ____ ____ ____ ____ ____ ____ and
714 39,403 71,829   168 107,943 319   407   840   2,387

____ ____ ____ 　 ____ ____ ____ ____ ____ ____ ____ ____
169 96,657 5,709   91,161 492 2,688 6,680 9,526 1,694 713 28,224

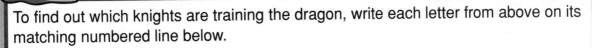

Name _____   Date _____

Doing the Limbo

Multiply.

1.   414
   x 222
   _____

2.   1,221
   x   344
   _____

3.   231
   x 132
   _____

4.   3,321
   x   230
   _____

5.   122
   x 244
   _____

6.   2,331
   x   313
   _____

7.   323
   x 202
   _____

8.   4,104
   x   221
   _____

9.   312
   x 313
   _____

10.   1,441
    x   121
   _____

Name _____ Date _____

That's a Wrap!

Solve.

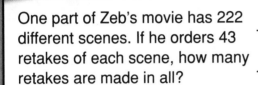

1

One part of Zeb's movie has 222 different scenes. If he orders 43 retakes of each scene, how many retakes are made in all?

_____ retakes

2

Zeb visits 111 cities to promote his new film. If he autographs 135 movie posters at each stop, how many posters does he sign in all?

_____ posters

3

Zeb travels 1,122 miles one week promoting the new film. If he travels that number of miles during each of 14 weeks, how many miles does he travel in all?

_____ miles

4

At one promotion stop, 4,321 fans gather to take photos of Zeb. If each fan takes 11 photos, how many photos are taken in all?

_____ photos

5

Some movie theaters are giving away tickets to promote the new movie. If 132 theaters give away 3,102 tickets each, how many tickets are given away in all?

_____ tickets

Name _____ Date _____

Bunch of Balloons

Multiply.

1
14
x 7

C

2
161
x 6

O

3
17
x 8

U

4
1,112
x 5

N

5
109
x 7

R

6
2,013
x 4

A

7
342
x 3

E

8
1,711
x 6

P

9
454
x 2

I

10
2,241
x 4

P

What animal would make a good balloon popper?

To answer the clown's question, write each letter from above on its matching numbered line below.

____   ____   ____   ____   ____   ____   ____   ____   ____
8,052   8,964   966   763   98   136   10,266   908   5,560   1,026

Yo-Yo Champ?

Multiply. Lightly shade each yo-yo that has a matching product. Two products will
not match the products on the yo-yos.

1.　　25 　　x 13	2.　　3,447 　　x　 12	3.　　116 　　x 51	4.　　28 　　x 13
5.　　446 　　x　20	6.　　29 　　x 13	7.　　1,013 　　x　 37	8.　　324 　　x 23
		9.　　15 　　x 16	10.　　1,113 　　x　 63

377
K

5,916
C

250
N

41,364
A

70,119
B

7,452
E

148,461
D

325
M

364
O

8,920
C

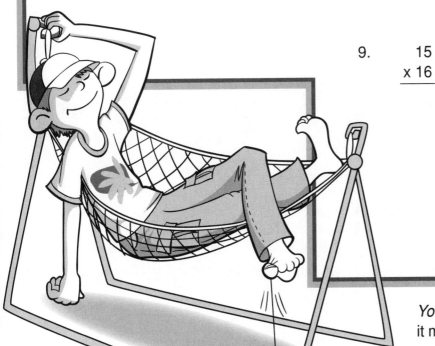

Yo-yo is a Filipino word. To find out what
it means, write the letters of the shaded
yo-yos, from bottom to top, on the lines
below.

___ ___ ___ ___ ___　___ ___ ___ ___

Target Toss

Multiply. Cross off each matching product on a can. Two products will not be used.

1. 218 x 114	2. 2,181 x 141

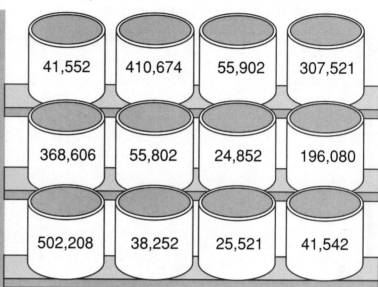

41,552	410,674	55,902	307,521
368,606	55,802	24,852	196,080
502,208	38,252	25,521	41,542

3. 3,262 x 113	4. 371 x 112

5. 181 x 141	6. 1,140 x 172

7. 3,394 x 121	8. 292 x 131

9. 462 x 121	10. 2,242 x 224

Name _____ Date _____

Good Luck Charms

Solve.

1. Before the contest, each contestant is allowed 35 warm-up shots. If there are 13 contestants, how many warm-up shots will be taken in all?

   _____ warm-up shots

Hoop-Shooting Contest
TODAY

2. Trevor always dribbles the ball 12 times before he attempts a free throw. If he attempts 145 free throws, how many times does he dribble the ball in all?

   _____ dribbles

3. If Trevor makes 28 layups in one minute, how many layups will he make in 112 minutes?

   _____ layups

4. During the contest, the contestants make 1,632 three-pointers in all. What is the total point value of these shots?

   _____ points

5. Fourteen large bags of candy were sold during the contest. If each bag contained 2,013 pieces of candy, how many pieces of candy were sold in all?

   _____ pieces

Name _____ Date _____

Airborne!

Multiply.

1. 476
    x 3

2. 694
    x 7

3. 548
    x 9

4. 378
    x 6

5. 819
    x 6

6. 753
    x 4

7. 3,406
    x   5

8. 6,943
    x   7

9. 1,892
    x   8

10. 4,263
    x   9

11. 7,544
    x   7

12. 9,573
    x   8

Honey Lover

Multiply.

1. 94
    x 75

2. 29
    x 43

3. 36
    x 78

4. 58
    x 24

5. 456
    x 39

6. 287
    x 33

7. 506
    x 88

8. 8,453
    x   36

9. 5,640
    x   44

10. 4,729
    x   63

Multiplication: more than one regrouping 27

Going Once, Going Twice, Sold!

Multiply.

1.   898
     x 207
	2. 3,918
	     x 454
		3. 924
		     x 786
			4. 6,401
			     x 395

5.   329
     x 586
	6. 4,151
	     x 309
		7. 592
		     x 816
			8. 3,627
			     x 225

To learn the amount of the final bid, subtract the sum of the products of the odd-numbered problems from the sum of the products of the even-numbered problems.

The final bid was $_____.

AUCTION

Grape-Picking Time

Solve.

1. The grape pickers filled a basket with six large bunches of grapes. If there are 128 grapes in each bunch, how many grapes are in the basket?

   _____ grapes

2. There are 1,574 grape pickers in the vineyards. If each worker picks 58 bunches of grapes, how many bunches of grapes will be picked in all?

   _____ bunches

3. If there are 22 rows of grapevines in each vineyard and there are 37 vineyards, how many rows of grapevines are there in all?

   _____ rows

4. The harvesters drink an average of 867 gallons of water each day. If these workers pick grapes for 112 days, how many gallons of water will be needed?

   _____ gallons

5. One vineyard has 1,425 vines. If there are 215 bunches of grapes on each vine, how many bunches are there in all?

   _____ bunches

Box the Bananas

Divide. If the quotient is more than 5, shade the bananas to show the path.

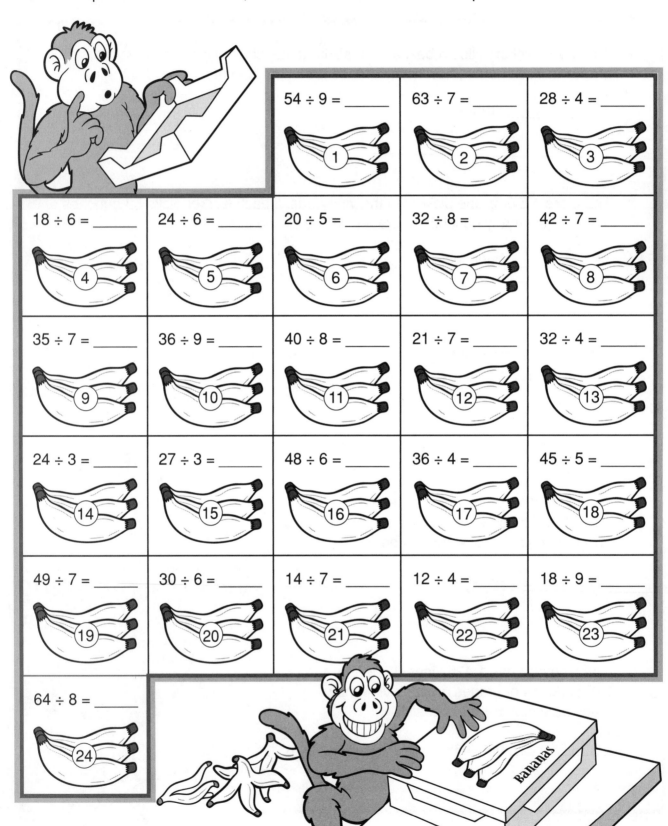

$54 \div 9 =$ _____ 1

$63 \div 7 =$ _____ 2

$28 \div 4 =$ _____ 3

$18 \div 6 =$ _____ 4

$24 \div 6 =$ _____ 5

$20 \div 5 =$ _____ 6

$32 \div 8 =$ _____ 7

$42 \div 7 =$ _____ 8

$35 \div 7 =$ _____ 9

$36 \div 9 =$ _____ 10

$40 \div 8 =$ _____ 11

$21 \div 7 =$ _____ 12

$32 \div 4 =$ _____ 13

$24 \div 3 =$ _____ 14

$27 \div 3 =$ _____ 15

$48 \div 6 =$ _____ 16

$36 \div 4 =$ _____ 17

$45 \div 5 =$ _____ 18

$49 \div 7 =$ _____ 19

$30 \div 6 =$ _____ 20

$14 \div 7 =$ _____ 21

$12 \div 4 =$ _____ 22

$18 \div 9 =$ _____ 23

$64 \div 8 =$ _____ 24

Name _____   Date _____

Roll the Presses!

Divide.

A $60 \div 3 =$ _____ $600 \div 3 =$ _____ $6{,}000 \div 3 =$ _____ $60{,}000 \div 3 =$ _____	**B** $540 \div 6 =$ _____ $5{,}400 \div 6 =$ _____ $54{,}000 \div 6 =$ _____ $540{,}000 \div 6 =$ _____	**C** $810 \div 9 =$ _____ $8{,}100 \div 9 =$ _____ $81{,}000 \div 9 =$ _____ $810{,}000 \div 9 =$ _____

D $420 \div 7 =$ _____ $4{,}200 \div 7 =$ _____ $42{,}000 \div 7 =$ _____ $420{,}000 \div 7 =$ _____	**E** $480 \div 8 =$ _____ $4{,}800 \div 8 =$ _____ $48{,}000 \div 8 =$ _____ $480{,}000 \div 8 =$ _____	**F** $720 \div 9 =$ _____ $7{,}200 \div 9 =$ _____ $72{,}000 \div 9 =$ _____ $720{,}000 \div 9 =$ _____

G $150 \div 50 =$ _____ $1{,}500 \div 50 =$ _____ $15{,}000 \div 50 =$ _____ $150{,}000 \div 50 =$ _____	**H** $280 \div 40 =$ _____ $2{,}800 \div 40 =$ _____ $28{,}000 \div 40 =$ _____ $280{,}000 \div 40 =$ _____

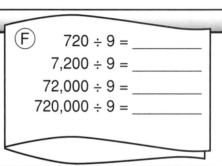

Name _____   Date _____

Guitar Guys

Shade the box that has the
correct estimated quotient.

1. 786 ÷ 2	40	**R**	400	**K**
2. 297 ÷ 6	500	**O**	50	**S**
3. 421 ÷ 7	6	**L**	60	**N**
4. 225 ÷ 5	4	**A**	40	**I**
5. 710 ÷ 8	900	**T**	90	**E**
6. 368 ÷ 4	90	**I**	9	**F**
7. 645 ÷ 9	70	**P**	7	**M**
8. 948 ÷ 3	300	**Z**	30	**A**
9. 234 ÷ 4	60	**M**	6	**D**
10. 814 ÷ 8	100	**C**	10	**H**
11. 161 ÷ 8	200	**W**	20	**E**
12. 393 ÷ 5	80	**S**	800	**B**

What did the guitars say to the guitarists?
To solve the riddle, write the letter from each shaded box above on its matching
numbered line below.

__ __ __ __   ON   __O__EO__ __   YOUR OWN   __ __ __ __!
7 4 10 1   12 9 3 11   2 6 8 5

Math Practice Pages • ©The Mailbox® Books • TEC61123 • Key p. 90

Name _____   Date _____

Let's Make Pizza! ___

Estimate the quotient on each pizza slice at the right.
Then cut out each slice and glue it to its matching pan.

Quotients from 100 to 499

Quotients from 500 to 900

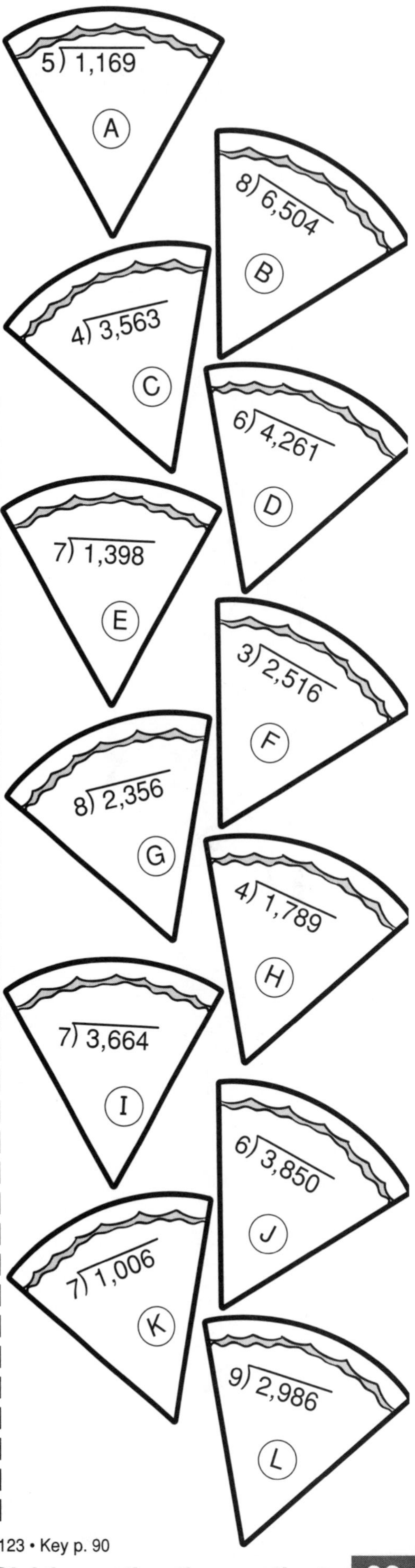

A $5\overline{)1,169}$

B $8\overline{)6,504}$

C $4\overline{)3,563}$

D $6\overline{)4,261}$

E $7\overline{)1,398}$

F $3\overline{)2,516}$

G $8\overline{)2,356}$

H $4\overline{)1,789}$

I $7\overline{)3,664}$

J $6\overline{)3,850}$

K $7\overline{)1,006}$

L $9\overline{)2,986}$

Name _____ Date _____

Up, Up, and Away!

Divide.
Cross off the quotient
on the basket.

A $6\overline{)78}$

B $2\overline{)92}$

C $8\overline{)96}$

D $4\overline{)72}$

E $3\overline{)78}$

F $6\overline{)966}$

G $5\overline{)600}$

H $8\overline{)808}$

I $7\overline{)847}$

J $2\overline{)684}$

K $5\overline{)7,850}$

L $6\overline{)9,378}$

M $3\overline{)6,594}$

N $4\overline{)8,496}$

O $7\overline{)9,884}$

120	46	342	161
13	1,563	1,412	12
2,198	1,570	26	18
121	101	2,124	

Stew For Supper

Divide.

① $8\overline{)34}$ = N

② $5\overline{)78}$ = H

③ $7\overline{)419}$ = E

④ $9\overline{)539}$ = B

⑤ $8\overline{)4,225}$ = I

⑥ $9\overline{)6,509}$ = T

⑦ $3\overline{)76}$ = T

⑧ $6\overline{)76}$ = A

⑨ $5\overline{)413}$ = S

⑩ $7\overline{)6,747}$ = E

⑪ $6\overline{)83}$ = H

⑫ $8\overline{)95}$ = I

⑬ $8\overline{)613}$ = R

⑭ $6\overline{)1,437}$ = Y

How can a man tell he's eating rabbit stew?

To answer the riddle, write each letter from above on its matching numbered line below.

___ ___ ___ ___ ___
59 R8   239 R3   25 R1   13 R5   59 R6

" ___ ___ ___ ___ ___ "   ___ ___   ___ ___ !
15 R3 12 R4 76 R5 963 R6 82 R3   528 R1 4 R2   11 R7 723 R2

Name _____ Date _____

Breakfast Bites

Solve.

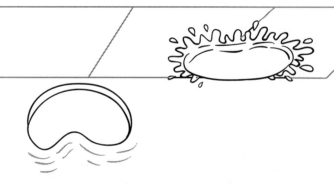

1. Carly likes Fruit Ring-Os for breakfast. One box makes 46 bowls of cereal. If she eats two bowls of cereal each day, how long will it take her to eat all the cereal in the box?

_____

2. Corey has 45 eggs. If he uses three eggs to make one omelet, how many omelets can he make with the eggs?

_____

3. Carly and Corey are using 154 chocolate chips to make pancakes. If they are the only ones who eat the pancakes and they each have the same amount, how many chocolate chips will each person eat?

_____

4. Carly loves bacon. If five pieces of bacon have a total of 80 calories, how many calories are in each piece?

_____

5. Corey and two friends are taste-testing 327 types of cereal. If they each taste an equal number of cereals, how many does each person taste-test?

_____

6. Carly and Corey are spreading seven pounds of butter on 1,043 pieces of toast. How many pieces of toast can they butter with one pound?

_____

Name _____   Date _____

Superhero Cleaners

Solve.

 1. Mr. Wash has 17 superhero capes to clean. If two capes will fit on one hanger, how many hangers will he need?

_____

 2. Mr. Wash is washing 86 superhero masks. Only nine masks fit in his washing machine at one time. How many loads of masks will he wash?

_____

 3. Super Sally wants to have 283 costumes cleaned. She can carry only nine costumes into the cleaners at one time. How many trips will she need to make to bring in all the costumes?

_____

4. Mr. Wash has 355 boxes of Supersoft dryer sheets. If he uses seven boxes each week, how many weeks will it take him to use all 355 boxes?

_____

5. Mr. Wash's supersize clothesline can hold six capes at one time. If he has 3,772 capes to dry, how many clotheslines will he need?

_____

 6. Mr. Wash has cleaned 2,452 costumes. If he can fit three clean costumes in one plastic bag, how many bags will he need?

_____

Chips 'n' Salsa

Divide.

1. $46\overline{)2,300}$

2. $13\overline{)156}$

3. $28\overline{)112}$

4. $97\overline{)194}$

5. $23\overline{)1,196}$

6. $89\overline{)5,874}$

7. $35\overline{)1,960}$

8. $95\overline{)570}$

9. $14\overline{)868}$

10. $39\overline{)2,340}$

11. $31\overline{)1,178}$

12. $39\overline{)897}$

13. $80\overline{)56,000}$

14. $34\overline{)41,888}$

15. $27\overline{)5,697}$

Division: no remainder

Math Practice Pages • ©The Mailbox® Books • TEC61123 • Key p. 91

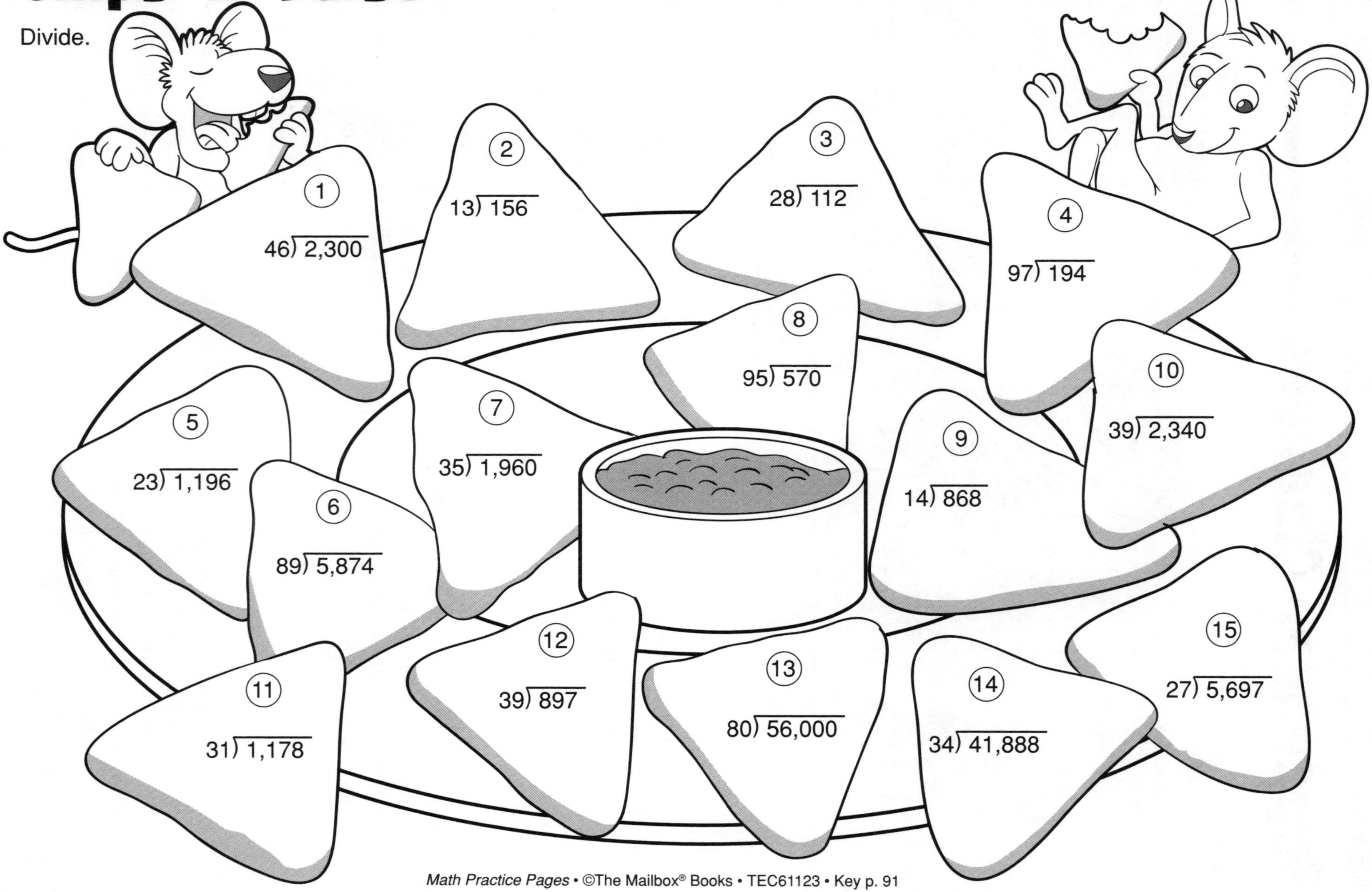

Magic Hat

Divide. Write the remainder for each problem in its matching box below.
If your answers are correct, the sum of each row, column, and diagonal will be 34.

(1) $15\overline{)107}$ (2) $12\overline{)139}$ (3) $15\overline{)125}$ (4) $12\overline{)136}$ (5) $17\overline{)118}$

(6) $43\overline{)96}$ (7) $11\overline{)135}$ (8) $29\overline{)156}$ (9) $16\overline{)108}$

(10) $22\overline{)123}$ (11) $74\overline{)4{,}663}$ (12) $51\overline{)1{,}340}$

(13) $75\overline{)4{,}809}$ (14) $73\overline{)4{,}607}$

(15) $38\overline{)2{,}561}$ (16) $12\overline{)62{,}082}$

5	7	1	10
3	6	8	14
13	16	2	9
4	15	12	11

Name _____ Date _____

Putting Around

Divide.

1. $31\overline{)142}$ 2. $51\overline{)130}$ 3. $12\overline{)139}$ 4. $33\overline{)127}$

5. $28\overline{)5,939}$ 6. $69\overline{)9,109}$ 7. $41\overline{)6,040}$ 8. $61\overline{)3,420}$

9. $27\overline{)15,295}$ 10. $38\overline{)62,004}$

11. $45\overline{)16,000}$ 12. $56\overline{)42,081}$

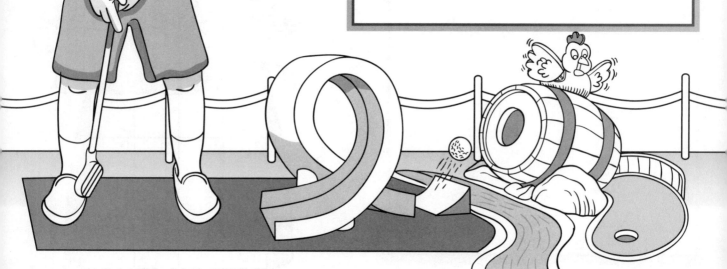

Name _____ Date _____

Toss 'em in the Bin!

Divide.

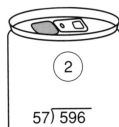

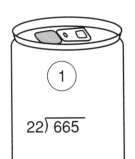
1

$22\overline{)665}$

2

$57\overline{)596}$

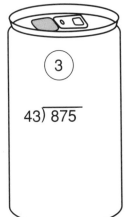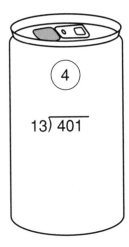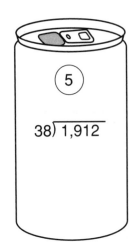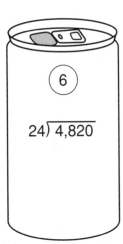
3

$43\overline{)875}$

4

$13\overline{)401}$

5

$38\overline{)1,912}$

6

$24\overline{)4,820}$

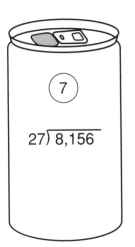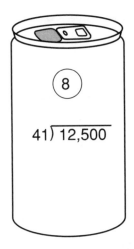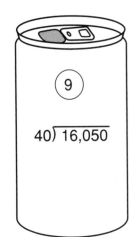
7

$27\overline{)8,156}$

8

$41\overline{)12,500}$

9

$40\overline{)16,050}$

10

$35\overline{)26,629}$

Name _____ Date _____

Heading Home

Circle each problem that is solved correctly.
Connect the circled problems to show the path.

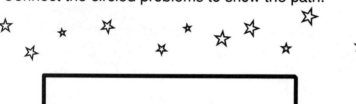

$$\begin{array}{r} 30 \text{ R}31 \\ 34\overline{)711} \end{array}$$

$$\begin{array}{r} 20 \text{ R}8 \\ 37\overline{)748} \end{array}$$

$$\begin{array}{r} 50 \text{ R}5 \\ 54\overline{)3,245} \end{array}$$

$$\begin{array}{r} 10 \text{ R}2 \\ 55\overline{)562} \end{array}$$

$$\begin{array}{r} 300 \text{ R}13 \\ 29\overline{)8,713} \end{array}$$

$$\begin{array}{r} 203 \text{ R}5 \\ 38\overline{)7,719} \end{array}$$

$$\begin{array}{r} 420 \text{ R}18 \\ 22\overline{)9,258} \end{array}$$

$$\begin{array}{r} 108 \\ 41\overline{)4,428} \end{array}$$

$$\begin{array}{r} 3,012 \text{ R}20 \\ 32\overline{)96,414} \end{array}$$

$$\begin{array}{r} 1,070 \text{ R}31 \\ 35\overline{)37,831} \end{array}$$

$$\begin{array}{r} 4,077 \text{ R}2 \\ 12\overline{)48,926} \end{array}$$

$$\begin{array}{r} 2,006 \text{ R}29 \\ 43\overline{)86,287} \end{array}$$

WELCOME HOME!

Name _____ Date _____

Farm Fresh!

Solve.

1. Farmer Ted puts 52 ears of corn in each crate. If he picks 421 ears of corn, how many crates will he need? _____

2. There are 11 tractors on the farm that are used to plow 1,320 acres of land. If each tractor is used to plow the same amount of land, how many acres does each tractor plow?

_____

3. The horses on the farm eat 1,848 pounds of hay. There are 22 horses, and each horse eats the same amount of hay. How many pounds of hay does each horse eat?

_____

4. Farmer Ted grows 13 different types of tomatoes for a total of 2,275 tomatoes. If he grows the same amount of each type, how many tomatoes of each type does Farmer Ted grow?

_____

5. There are 51,457 apples in the orchard. If 25 apples fit in one basket, how many baskets will Farmer Ted need for all his apples?

_____

6. Farmer Ted sells 37,116 cartons of eggs each year. If he sells the same number of cartons each month, how many cartons of eggs does he sell each month?

_____

Batting Practice

Circle the two equivalent fractions on each ball.

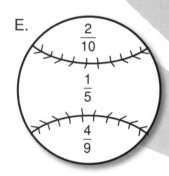

A.
$\frac{1}{6}$
$\frac{3}{12}$
$\frac{5}{30}$

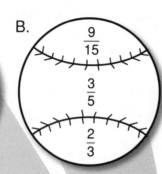

B.
$\frac{9}{15}$
$\frac{3}{5}$
$\frac{2}{3}$

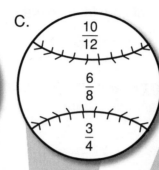

C.
$\frac{10}{12}$
$\frac{6}{8}$
$\frac{3}{4}$

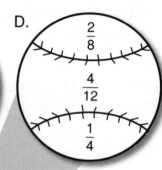

D.
$\frac{2}{8}$
$\frac{4}{12}$
$\frac{1}{4}$

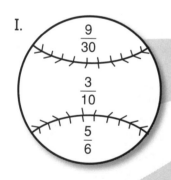

E.
$\frac{2}{10}$
$\frac{1}{5}$
$\frac{4}{9}$

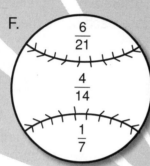

F.
$\frac{6}{21}$
$\frac{4}{14}$
$\frac{1}{7}$

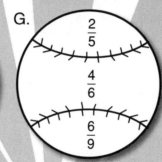

G.
$\frac{2}{5}$
$\frac{4}{6}$
$\frac{6}{9}$

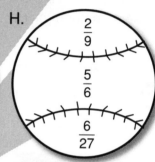

H.
$\frac{2}{9}$
$\frac{5}{6}$
$\frac{6}{27}$

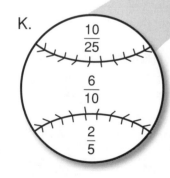

I.
$\frac{9}{30}$
$\frac{3}{10}$
$\frac{5}{6}$

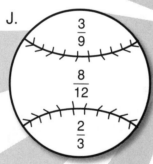

J.
$\frac{3}{9}$
$\frac{8}{12}$
$\frac{2}{3}$

K.
$\frac{10}{25}$
$\frac{6}{10}$
$\frac{2}{5}$

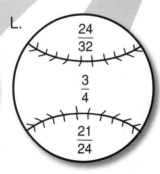

L.
$\frac{24}{32}$
$\frac{3}{4}$
$\frac{21}{24}$

Name _____ Date _____

Playtime

Shade the box that makes each comparison true.

1.	$\frac{3}{8}$ <	$\frac{5}{8}$ H	$\frac{2}{8}$ G
2.	$\frac{1}{3}$ <	$\frac{1}{7}$ C	$\frac{2}{5}$ W
3.	$\frac{7}{15}$ >	$\frac{11}{15}$ O	$\frac{4}{15}$ A
4.	$\frac{5}{7}$ <	$\frac{7}{9}$ E	$\frac{1}{3}$ H
5.	$\frac{3}{6}$ >	$\frac{15}{18}$ K	$\frac{4}{9}$ E
6.	$\frac{4}{11}$ <	$\frac{3}{11}$ M	$\frac{9}{10}$ W
7.	$\frac{6}{14}$ >	$\frac{5}{14}$ T	$\frac{13}{14}$ S
8.	$\frac{3}{4}$ >	$\frac{7}{16}$ O	$\frac{7}{8}$ A

9.	$\frac{3}{4}$ >	$\frac{7}{8}$ P	$\frac{1}{4}$ R
10.	$\frac{5}{10}$ =	$\frac{3}{6}$ D	$\frac{2}{3}$ B
11.	$\frac{7}{12}$ >	$\frac{3}{4}$ F	$\frac{1}{2}$ A
12.	$\frac{5}{9}$ >	$\frac{4}{9}$ E	$\frac{8}{9}$ U
13.	$\frac{11}{20}$ <	$\frac{7}{20}$ T	$\frac{17}{20}$ S
14.	$\frac{3}{5}$ <	$\frac{2}{5}$ N	$\frac{4}{5}$ L
15.	$\frac{3}{10}$ >	$\frac{5}{20}$ L	$\frac{7}{8}$ J
16.	$\frac{5}{8}$ <	$\frac{7}{8}$ L	$\frac{3}{8}$ V

What is a shark's favorite game?

To answer the riddle, write each shaded letter from above on its matching numbered line below.

___ ___ ___ ___ ___ ___ ___   ___ ___ ___   ___ ___ ___ ___ ___ ___
13 6 11 15 16 8 2   7 1 5   14 12 3 10 4 9

Name _____ Date _____

Want a Gumball?

Write each answer in its simplest form.

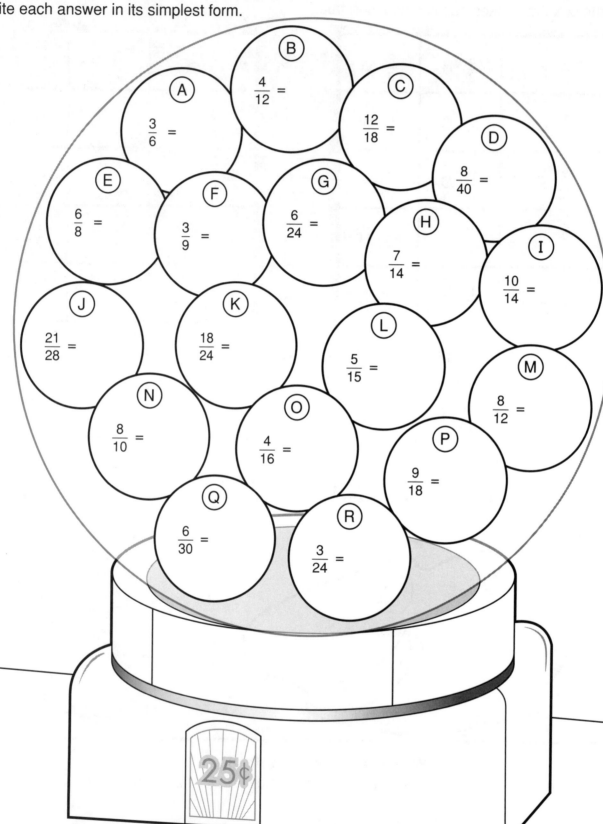

A $\frac{3}{6} =$

B $\frac{4}{12} =$

C $\frac{12}{18} =$

D $\frac{8}{40} =$

E $\frac{6}{8} =$

F $\frac{3}{9} =$

G $\frac{6}{24} =$

H $\frac{7}{14} =$

I $\frac{10}{14} =$

J $\frac{21}{28} =$

K $\frac{18}{24} =$

L $\frac{5}{15} =$

M $\frac{8}{12} =$

N $\frac{8}{10} =$

O $\frac{4}{16} =$

P $\frac{9}{18} =$

Q $\frac{6}{30} =$

R $\frac{3}{24} =$

25¢

Name _____   Date _____

Salty Snack

If the fraction is closest to 0, circle it.
If the fraction is closest to $\frac{1}{2}$, draw a triangle around it.
If the fraction is closest to 1, draw a box around it.

Rock-Solid Construction Company

Add or subtract. Write each answer in its simplest form.

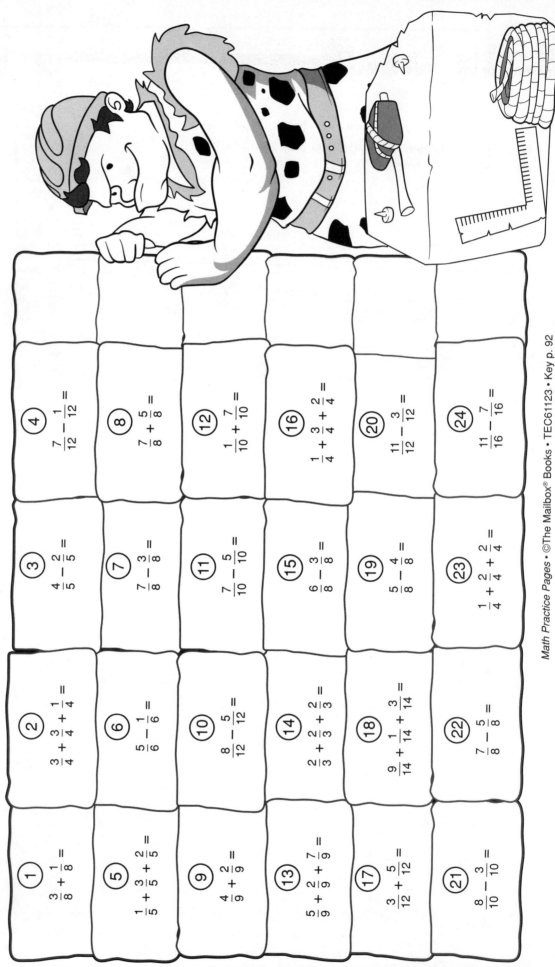

1
$$\frac{3}{8} + \frac{1}{8} =$$

2
$$\frac{3}{4} + \frac{3}{4} + \frac{1}{4} =$$

3
$$\frac{4}{5} - \frac{2}{5} =$$

4
$$\frac{7}{12} - \frac{1}{12} =$$

5
$$\frac{1}{5} + \frac{3}{5} + \frac{2}{5} =$$

6
$$\frac{5}{6} - \frac{1}{6} =$$

7
$$\frac{7}{8} - \frac{3}{8} =$$

8
$$\frac{7}{8} + \frac{5}{8} =$$

9
$$\frac{4}{9} + \frac{2}{9} =$$

10
$$\frac{8}{12} - \frac{5}{12} =$$

11
$$\frac{7}{10} - \frac{5}{10} =$$

12
$$\frac{1}{10} + \frac{7}{10} =$$

13
$$\frac{5}{9} + \frac{2}{9} + \frac{7}{9} =$$

14
$$\frac{2}{3} + \frac{2}{3} + \frac{2}{3} =$$

15
$$\frac{6}{8} - \frac{3}{8} =$$

16
$$\frac{1}{4} + \frac{3}{4} + \frac{2}{4} =$$

17
$$\frac{3}{12} + \frac{5}{12} =$$

18
$$\frac{9}{14} + \frac{1}{14} + \frac{3}{14} =$$

19
$$\frac{5}{8} - \frac{4}{8} =$$

20
$$\frac{11}{12} - \frac{3}{12} =$$

21
$$\frac{8}{10} - \frac{3}{10} =$$

22
$$\frac{7}{8} - \frac{5}{8} =$$

23
$$\frac{1}{4} + \frac{2}{4} + \frac{2}{4} =$$

24
$$\frac{11}{16} - \frac{7}{16} =$$

Fractions: adding and subtracting like fractions

Name _____   Date _____

Scrub-a-dub-dub

Add or subtract. Write each answer in its simplest form.

1. $\dfrac{7}{8}$
    $+\ \dfrac{1}{4}$

2. $\dfrac{5}{12}$
    $-\ \dfrac{1}{8}$

3. $\dfrac{1}{3}$
    $+\ \dfrac{5}{6}$

4. $\dfrac{3}{4}$
    $\dfrac{5}{8}$
    $+\ \dfrac{3}{4}$

5. $\dfrac{4}{10}$
    $-\ \dfrac{1}{4}$

6. $\dfrac{5}{9}$
    $-\ \dfrac{1}{2}$

7. $\dfrac{1}{2}$
    $+\ \dfrac{3}{4}$

8. $\dfrac{2}{3}$
    $+\ \dfrac{5}{6}$

9. $\dfrac{1}{8}$
    $+\ \dfrac{3}{4}$

10. $\dfrac{2}{3}$
    $-\ \dfrac{3}{5}$

11. $\dfrac{3}{4}$
    $-\ \dfrac{1}{12}$

12. $\dfrac{1}{8}$
    $\dfrac{1}{2}$
    $+\ \dfrac{3}{4}$

How many towels will it take to dry the dog?
To find out, add together the answers to problems 1, 4, 7, and 8.

_____ towels

Name _____   Date _____

Computer Buddies

Solve. Write each answer in its simplest form.

1. Jay checks his email every day. On Monday, $\frac{2}{7}$ of the messages in his inbox are from friends and $\frac{4}{7}$ are from relatives. What fraction of the messages is from friends and relatives?

_____

2. Alex uses a computer at home and another one at school. He uses his home computer $\frac{5}{8}$ of the time and a school computer $\frac{3}{8}$ of the time. How much more time does he spend on his home computer than the one at school?

_____

3. While playing a computer game, Jay earned $\frac{8}{15}$ of the total points. Alex earned $\frac{6}{15}$ of the total points. What fraction of the points did they earn together?

_____

4. Alex and Jay each want to buy a new computer. Alex has $\frac{3}{5}$ of the money he needs and Jay has $\frac{1}{5}$ of the money he needs. What fraction of the money does each boy still need?

_____

5. Companies donate $\frac{1}{10}$ of the school computers. The PTO buys $\frac{7}{10}$ of the computers. What fraction of the school computers are donated by companies or bought by the PTO?

_____

6. Jay uses $\frac{9}{12}$ of his computer time at home for schoolwork and $\frac{1}{12}$ for email. How much longer is his schoolwork time than his email time?

_____

Name _____ Date _____

Deep Dish

Solve. Write each answer in its simplest form.

1. One-half of the pies in the baker's oven are apple and $\frac{1}{4}$ are strawberry. What fraction of the pies is either apple or strawberry?

   _____

2. Nicole is eating $\frac{1}{6}$ of a blueberry pie she bought at a bakery. Eric is eating $\frac{3}{8}$ of the pie. How much of the pie are they eating in all?

   _____

3. Nicole's mom is eating $\frac{1}{5}$ of a blackberry pie. Her mom's friends are eating $\frac{5}{8}$ of it. How much of the pie is being eaten?

   _____

4. After dinner at Nicole's house, there is $\frac{3}{8}$ of a peach pie left and $\frac{1}{3}$ of an apple pie left. How much more peach pie than apple pie is left?

   _____

5. Eric's piece of pie is $\frac{3}{4}$ inches thick. Nicole's piece of pie is $\frac{2}{3}$ inches thick. How much thicker is Eric's piece than Nicole's?

   _____

6. The baker bakes $\frac{1}{2}$ of the pies for the day. His helper bakes $\frac{1}{3}$ of the day's pies. How many of the pies have they baked?

   _____

Name _____ Date _____

Under the Weather

Add or subtract. Write each answer in its simplest form. Cross out the square with the matching answer below.

1. $2\frac{1}{8} + 2\frac{5}{8} =$

2. $9\frac{1}{12} + 1\frac{5}{12} =$

3. $5\frac{5}{6} - 1\frac{1}{6} =$

4. $3\frac{9}{10} - 1\frac{7}{10} =$

5. $2\frac{2}{9} + 4\frac{1}{9} =$

6. $2\frac{1}{6} + 3\frac{1}{6} =$

7. $6\frac{1}{10} + 3\frac{3}{10} =$

8. $2\frac{7}{8} - 1\frac{1}{8} =$

9. $3\frac{5}{6} - 1\frac{3}{6} =$

10. $8\frac{4}{6} - 5\frac{1}{6} =$

11. $4\frac{4}{8} + 1\frac{1}{8} + 2\frac{2}{8} =$

12. $6\frac{9}{15} + 2\frac{1}{15} + 1\frac{2}{15} =$

									$2\frac{1}{5}$
									L

$4\frac{1}{2}$	$4\frac{3}{4}$	$10\frac{2}{3}$	$4\frac{1}{6}$	$10\frac{1}{2}$	$4\frac{2}{3}$	$3\frac{1}{2}$	$2\frac{2}{5}$	$6\frac{1}{3}$	$8\frac{1}{3}$
T	**A**	**W**	**E**	**O**	**N**	**C**	**E**	**B**	**T**
$2\frac{1}{3}$	$9\frac{4}{5}$	$5\frac{1}{12}$	$1\frac{3}{4}$	$9\frac{3}{5}$	$9\frac{2}{5}$	$1\frac{3}{8}$	$7\frac{7}{8}$	$2\frac{1}{2}$	$5\frac{1}{3}$
A	**D**	**M**	**F**	**E**	**G**	**N**	**S**	**T**	**U**

What do you give a sick bird?
To find out, write the letters in the remaining squares in order on the lines below.

" __ __ __ __ __ __ __ __ __ "!

Thirst Quencher

Add or subtract. Write each answer in its simplest form.

1. $2\frac{1}{5}$
  $+ 5\frac{1}{3}$

2. $3\frac{3}{4}$
  $- 1\frac{1}{2}$

3. $3\frac{2}{3}$
  $+ 5\frac{8}{9}$

4. $9\frac{5}{6}$
  $- 2\frac{1}{2}$

5. $3\frac{7}{8}$
  $+ 5\frac{1}{4}$

6. $3\frac{5}{6}$
  $- 1\frac{1}{2}$

7. $5\frac{1}{2}$
  $+ 3\frac{3}{4}$

8. $8\frac{2}{3}$
  $- 5\frac{1}{6}$

9. $5\frac{7}{9}$
  $+ 7\frac{1}{3}$

10. $10\frac{7}{8}$
  $- 4\frac{1}{4}$

SUPERSIZE IT, PLEASE.

Big-Game Hunter

Add or subtract. Write each answer in its simplest form.

1. $6\frac{7}{12}$
    $+\,3\frac{2}{3}$

2. $5\frac{7}{10}$
    $+\,2\frac{3}{5}$

3. $5\frac{7}{8}$
    $-\,1\frac{3}{4}$

4. $7\frac{4}{5}$
    $-\,2\frac{1}{10}$

5. $4\frac{5}{6}$
    $+\,6\frac{5}{12}$

6. $7\frac{5}{6}$
    $+\,4\frac{5}{8}$

7. $7\frac{4}{9}$
    $-\,6\frac{2}{3}$

8. $9\frac{9}{16}$
    $-\,6\frac{3}{8}$

9. $12\frac{1}{6}$
    $-\,5\frac{5}{12}$

10. $4\frac{1}{4}$
    $3\frac{5}{8}$
    $+\,2\frac{5}{8}$

11. $2\frac{9}{10}$
    $3\frac{2}{5}$
    $+\,1\frac{1}{5}$

12. $6\frac{5}{6}$
    $-\,6\frac{1}{2}$

Pets Galore

Solve. Write each answer in its simplest form.

1. On Monday, Mr. Kelly restocked $2\frac{1}{4}$ shelves with pet food. On Tuesday, he restocked $4\frac{1}{4}$ shelves. How many shelves did he restock in all?

   _____

2. To clean the hamsters' cages, Mr. Kelly mixes $6\frac{3}{8}$ cups of water with $3\frac{3}{8}$ cups of cleaner. How much more water does he mix than cleaner?

   _____

3. During the week, Mr. Kelly spent $4\frac{1}{9}$ hours grooming dogs. Over the weekend, he spent $1\frac{7}{9}$ hours grooming dogs. How much time did Mr. Kelly spend grooming dogs in all?

   _____

4. Mr. Kelly sold $6\frac{1}{4}$ boxes of squeaky toys. He sold $6\frac{2}{4}$ boxes of chew toys as well. How many boxes of toys did he sell in all?

   _____

5. The store's water bowl for pets has $4\frac{3}{8}$ cups of water in it. The food bowl has $1\frac{1}{8}$ cups of food in it. How much more water is there than food?

   _____

6. One customer is buying a leash that is $8\frac{3}{10}$ feet long. A second customer is buying a leash that is $3\frac{1}{10}$ feet shorter than the first customer's. How long is the second leash?

   _____

Math Practice Pages · ©The Mailbox® Books · TEC61123 · Key p. 93

Name _____ Date _____

Polar Pops

Solve. Write each answer in its simplest form.

1. Pete uses $2\frac{3}{8}$ scoops of vanilla ice cream and $2\frac{4}{5}$ scoops of strawberry ice cream to make a milk shake. How much ice cream does Pete use in all?

_____

2. When Pete checks the ice cream cones, he sees that $4\frac{3}{7}$ of the waffle cones are cracked and $2\frac{1}{3}$ of the sugar cones are cracked. How many more waffle cones than sugar cones are cracked?

_____

3. Ice cream sandwiches fill $3\frac{1}{3}$ shelves in the freezer. Ice cream cakes fill $8\frac{3}{4}$ shelves. How many more shelves are filled with ice cream cakes than ice cream sandwiches?

_____

4. Pete works for $1\frac{1}{2}$ hours before he takes a break. He then works for $3\frac{2}{3}$ more hours. How long does Pete work in all?

_____

5. Pete used $5\frac{1}{3}$ cartons of ice cream to fill orders for children. He used $1\frac{5}{6}$ cartons to fill orders for their parents. How many more cartons of ice cream have the kids eaten than the parents?

_____

6. Pete sold $6\frac{1}{4}$ boxes of ice cream bars on Thursday night. He sold $7\frac{1}{3}$ boxes on Friday night and $8\frac{1}{2}$ boxes on Saturday night. How many boxes of ice cream bars did Pete sell in all?

_____

Finish the Limerick

Multiply. Write each answer in its simplest form.

1. $\frac{1}{2} \times \frac{1}{2} =$

2. $\frac{7}{10} \times \frac{2}{3} =$

3. $\frac{2}{5} \times \frac{3}{7} =$

4. $\frac{1}{6} \times \frac{1}{3} =$

5. $\frac{1}{6} \times \frac{4}{5} =$

6. $\frac{7}{9} \times \frac{5}{6} =$

7. $\frac{3}{5} \times \frac{5}{8} =$

8. $\frac{2}{15} \times \frac{3}{4} =$

9. $\frac{2}{3} \times \frac{1}{4} =$

10. $\frac{1}{8} \times \frac{3}{4} =$

11. $\frac{3}{7} \times \frac{5}{8} =$

12. $\frac{2}{9} \times \frac{3}{7} =$

Code

$\frac{3}{8}$	= bought
$\frac{3}{32}$	= wear
$\frac{5}{8}$	= sold
$\frac{35}{54}$	= pants
$\frac{3}{4}$	= shirt
$\frac{6}{35}$	= France
$\frac{13}{56}$	= Spain
$\frac{1}{4}$	= once
$\frac{15}{56}$	= friends
$\frac{3}{10}$	= sell
$\frac{7}{15}$	= man
$\frac{1}{10}$	= pair
$\frac{2}{15}$	= hole
$\frac{2}{21}$	= dance
$\frac{1}{18}$	= tore
$\frac{1}{6}$	= something

To complete the poem, use the code. Write the words from the code on the matching numbered lines below. Some words will not be used.

There _____ was a young _____
            1   2

  from _____
             3

Who _____ a big _____ in his
          4   5

_____ .
     6

He _____ a new _____ ,
     7   8

So he'd have _____ to _____
         9   10

When he went with his _____ to a
              11

_____ .
     12

Name _____   Date _____

Something to Crow About

Multiply. Write each answer in its simplest form.

1. $\frac{1}{3} \times \frac{5}{6} =$ (S)   2. $\frac{4}{5} \times \frac{1}{2} =$ (I)

3. $\frac{1}{3} \times \frac{1}{2} =$ (E)   4. $\frac{5}{6} \times \frac{3}{4} =$ (M)

5. $\frac{1}{4} \times \frac{1}{5} =$ (O)   6. $\frac{2}{3} \times \frac{1}{4} =$ (E)

7. $\frac{3}{5} \times \frac{3}{5} =$ (N)   8. $\frac{1}{2} \times \frac{7}{8} =$ (C)

9. $\frac{1}{4} \times \frac{3}{8} =$ (D)   10. $\frac{2}{3} \times \frac{5}{8} =$ (H)

What animals tell the funniest jokes?

To solve the riddle, write each letter from above on its matching numbered line below.

" ___ ___ ___ ___ ___ ___ - ___ ___ ___ ___ "!
$\frac{7}{16}$ $\frac{1}{20}$ $\frac{5}{8}$ $\frac{1}{6}$ $\frac{3}{32}$ $\frac{2}{5}$ $\frac{5}{12}$ $\frac{1}{6}$ $\frac{9}{25}$ $\frac{5}{18}$

Big Catch

Multiply. Write each answer in its simplest form.

1. $\frac{1}{3} \times \frac{2}{3} =$

2. $\frac{3}{4} \times \frac{8}{9} =$

3. $\frac{1}{8} \times \frac{4}{5} =$

4. $\frac{4}{7} \times \frac{1}{5} =$

5. $\frac{1}{9} \times \frac{3}{5} =$

6. $\frac{1}{5} \times \frac{1}{2} =$

7. $\frac{5}{6} \times \frac{2}{3} =$

8. $\frac{2}{5} \times \frac{1}{4} =$

9. $\frac{3}{7} \times \frac{5}{6} =$

10. $\frac{2}{3} \times \frac{3}{4} =$

11. $\frac{1}{2} \times \frac{3}{10} =$

12. $\frac{3}{4} \times \frac{2}{9} =$

13. $\frac{7}{12} \times \frac{2}{3} =$

14. $\frac{9}{10} \times \frac{2}{3} =$

Name _____ Date _____

Who Struck It Rich?

Multiply. Write each answer in its simplest form. Shade the box with the matching answer to show the path.

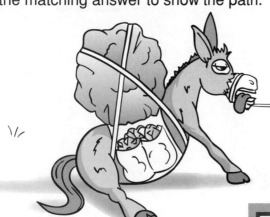

1. $\frac{1}{5} \times 7 =$

2. $\frac{1}{4} \times 9 =$

3. $\frac{3}{4} \times 6 =$

4. $\frac{1}{2} \times 4 =$

5. $\frac{2}{3} \times 4 =$

6. $\frac{3}{5} \times 5 =$

7. $6 \times \frac{2}{7} =$

8. $3 \times \frac{5}{8} =$

9. $2 \times \frac{7}{8} =$

10. $\frac{4}{5} \times 7 =$

11. $\frac{1}{3} \times 5 =$

12. $\frac{2}{9} \times 8 =$

13. $\frac{3}{10} \times 9 =$

14. $\frac{1}{8} \times 2 =$

15. $\frac{1}{6} \times 3 =$

$1\frac{2}{5}$	$\frac{7}{5}$	35	$5\frac{1}{7}$
$\frac{9}{4}$	$2\frac{1}{4}$	$4\frac{1}{9}$	36
$\frac{18}{4}$	$6\frac{3}{4}$	$4\frac{1}{2}$	$\frac{24}{3}$
$4\frac{1}{2}$	$2\frac{1}{4}$	$\frac{1}{8}$	2
$\frac{8}{3}$	6	$4\frac{2}{3}$	$2\frac{2}{3}$
$5\frac{3}{5}$	$\frac{25}{3}$	$\frac{15}{25}$	3
$6\frac{2}{7}$	$7\frac{1}{3}$	$1\frac{5}{7}$	$21\frac{1}{7}$
$8\frac{3}{5}$	$1\frac{7}{8}$	$3\frac{5}{8}$	$\frac{15}{24}$
$1\frac{3}{4}$	$2\frac{7}{8}$	$8\frac{2}{7}$	$\frac{14}{16}$
$5\frac{3}{5}$	$7\frac{4}{5}$	$35\frac{1}{4}$	$4\frac{5}{7}$
$5\frac{1}{3}$	$1\frac{2}{3}$	$3\frac{1}{5}$	$15\frac{1}{3}$
$8\frac{2}{9}$	$9\frac{1}{4}$	$1\frac{7}{9}$	$\frac{16}{72}$
$9\frac{3}{10}$	$3\frac{9}{10}$	$1\frac{7}{10}$	$2\frac{7}{10}$
$2\frac{1}{8}$	$8\frac{1}{2}$	$\frac{1}{4}$	16
18	$\frac{1}{2}$	$3\frac{1}{6}$	$6\frac{1}{3}$

| Mike | Malcolm | Marty | Mel |

A Whale of a Ride

Multiply. Write each answer in its simplest form.

  ① $\frac{1}{3}$ x 9 =   ② 10 x $\frac{1}{4}$ =   ③ $\frac{1}{4}$ x 7 =

  ④ $\frac{2}{5}$ x 7 =   ⑤ 5 x $\frac{3}{8}$ =   ⑥ $\frac{3}{5}$ x 2 =

  ⑦ $\frac{5}{6}$ x 6 =   ⑧ 3 x $\frac{1}{9}$ =   ⑨ $\frac{2}{7}$ x 14 =

  ⑩ 4 x $\frac{7}{8}$ =   ⑪ 8 x $\frac{3}{7}$ =   ⑫ $\frac{1}{5}$ x 12 =

  ⑬ $\frac{4}{5}$ x 6 =   ⑭ 3 x $\frac{1}{12}$ =   ⑮ $\frac{4}{9}$ x 4 =

  ⑯ 5 x $\frac{1}{10}$ =   ⑰ 15 x $\frac{2}{3}$ =   ⑱ $\frac{3}{4}$ x 8 =

Name _____   Date _____

Fancy Roper

Multiply. Write each answer in its simplest form.

(1) $\frac{5}{12} \times 1\frac{1}{2} =$ (2) $\frac{2}{5} \times 4\frac{1}{6} =$

(3) $\frac{1}{2} \times 1\frac{5}{8} =$ (4) $\frac{1}{4} \times 2\frac{1}{3} =$

(5) $\frac{3}{10} \times 5\frac{2}{3} =$ (6) $\frac{1}{7} \times 3\frac{5}{6} =$

(7) $\frac{1}{5} \times 6\frac{1}{8} =$ (8) $\frac{4}{5} \times 1\frac{3}{7} =$

(9) $\frac{1}{4} \times 3\frac{3}{5} =$ (10) $\frac{2}{9} \times 1\frac{4}{5} =$

(11) $\frac{1}{8} \times 2\frac{2}{5} =$ (12) $\frac{3}{4} \times 2\frac{1}{6} =$

(13) $\frac{3}{8} \times 4\frac{1}{3} =$ (14) $\frac{1}{9} \times 4\frac{1}{2} =$

Name _____ Date _____

Smile!

Multiply. Write each answer in its simplest form.

<table>
<tr>
<td>

① $6\frac{1}{4} \times 3\frac{1}{5} =$

</td>
<td>

② $1\frac{1}{7} \times 2\frac{1}{3} =$

</td>
</tr>
<tr>
<td>

③ $1\frac{1}{5} \times 2\frac{1}{2} =$

</td>
<td>

④ $3\frac{1}{9} \times 1\frac{1}{4} =$

</td>
</tr>
</table>

<table>
<tr>
<td>

⑤ $3\frac{1}{2} \times 2\frac{1}{7} =$

</td>
<td>

⑥ $2\frac{1}{6} \times 1\frac{1}{2} =$

</td>
<td>

⑦ $2\frac{1}{8} \times 1\frac{1}{3} =$

</td>
</tr>
</table>

<table>
<tr>
<td>

⑧ $1\frac{2}{9} \times 1\frac{7}{11} =$

</td>
<td>

⑨ $3\frac{3}{4} \times 2\frac{2}{5} =$

</td>
<td>

⑩ $5\frac{1}{6} \times 1\frac{1}{3} =$

</td>
<td>

⑪ $5\frac{1}{2} \times 1\frac{1}{3} =$

</td>
</tr>
<tr>
<td>

⑫ $8\frac{1}{8} \times 3\frac{1}{5} =$

</td>
<td>

⑬ $2\frac{6}{7} \times 2\frac{1}{10} =$

</td>
<td>

⑭ $2\frac{1}{7} \times 2\frac{1}{10} =$

</td>
<td>

⑮ $7\frac{1}{3} \times 1\frac{1}{8} =$

</td>
</tr>
</table>

Fractions: multiplying a mixed number by a mixed number

Name _____ Date _____

Shopping Spree

Solve. Write each answer in its simplest form.

1. Nick, Ty, Jessie, and Emma won a shopping spree at the mall. Each child received $\frac{1}{4}$ of the money. If each person spends $\frac{2}{5}$ of his or her money buying CDs, how much of the money will be spent on music?

   _____

2. Jessie and Emma are shopping for clothes. The clothes fill $3\frac{1}{4}$ shopping bags. If they empty $\frac{2}{5}$ of the bags, what part of the bags will they empty?

   _____

3. Nick and Ty each spend $\frac{1}{4}$ of their money in the arcade. They spend $\frac{4}{5}$ of the money playing Ultimate Street Skater II. How much of their money do they spend on that one game?

   _____

4. At the mall, $\frac{1}{3}$ of the people shopping are under the age of 15. Of that number, $\frac{3}{4}$ attend the same school as Emma. What fraction of the shoppers goes to Emma's school?

   _____

5. Fifteen of the stores in the mall sell clothes. Of the stores that sell clothes, $\frac{2}{3}$ of them sell only girls' clothes. How many of the mall's clothing stores sell only girls' clothes?

   _____

6. Nick and Ty are in the mall for $2\frac{1}{4}$ hours. Jessie and Emma are in the mall $1\frac{5}{6}$ times longer than the boys. How many hours are Jessie and Emma in the mall?

   _____

Name _____   Date _____

Get There Quick!

Write the decimal.

1. seven hundredths _____

2. two and three tenths _____

3. seven hundred fifteen thousandths _____

4. six tenths _____

5. three and six hundredths _____

6. eight thousandths _____

GNASHY McGNAW'S
DOG BONE FACTORY

Write the word name.

7. 67.98 _____

8. 1.8 _____

9. 0.007 _____

10. 1.375 _____

11. 1.2 _____

12. 5.02 _____

Write the value of the underlined digit.

13. 4.2 _____   14. 6.85 _____   15. 0.79 _____

16. 9.632 _____   17. 0.004 _____   18. 5.371 _____

19. 25.070 _____

20. 13.026 _____

21. 0.054 _____

22. 10.295 _____

23. 0.103 _____

24. 12.002 _____

Video Game Champ

Shade the box if the decimals are equivalent.
Connect the shaded boxes to show
   the path to the finish.

Start

0.2 and 0.20

0.800 and 0.8

1.30 and 1.3

0.5 and 0.05

8.9 and 8.09

0.03 and 0.30

6.09 and 6.9

0.3 and 0.30

6.05 and 6.050

1.05 and 1.050

0.72 and 0.702

Finish

6.40 and 6.4

2.08 and 2.080

0.41 and 0.410

0.700 and 0.7

1.550 and 1.55

7.50 and 7.5

0.35 and 0.035

0.7 and 0.07

0.44 and 0.04

0.9 and 9.0

Name _____ Date _____

Stampede!

Compare the decimals.
Shade the box of the correct comparison in each row.

#								
1	4.4 < 4.04	D	8.2 < 8.15	C	0.11 < 0.29	I
2	0.86 < 0.68	B	39.42 < 39.4	A	4.5 < 5.4	T
3	8.06 < 8.03	E	3.15 > 3.015	S	3.4 < 3.3	U
4	10.64 < 10.63	F	10.50 < 10.75	C	0.13 < 0.10	G
5	7.015 < 7.105	R	20.02 < 20.01	I	9.65 < 9.26	H
6	5.16 < 5.06	K	9.56 < 9.86	E	14.17 > 14.2	L
7	29.71 > 29.713	N	80.6 > 81.6	M	4.25 > 4.025	D
8	7.21 > 7.225	O	1.3 < 2.7	I	60.6 < 6.06	P
9	6.013 < 6.310	T	0.14 > 0.15	S	0.98 < 0.908	R
10	8.023 > 8.005	C	33.1 > 33.11	W	2.31 > 6.5	A
11	45.07 > 45.57	C	0.2 > 0.19	A	5.2 < 5.17	B
12	23.0 > 32.0	D	17.02 < 18.20	R	13.94 > 13.95	F
13	6.53 < 6.5	H	0.21 > 0.27	G	14.25 < 14.38	D
14	0.08 > 8.0	E	5.40 > 5.41	K	80.6 > 8.06	S

How can you prevent an elephant from charging?
To solve the riddle, write the letters in the shaded boxes from above in order on the lines below.

TAKE AWAY ___ ___ ___   ___ ___ ___ ___ ___ ___   ___ ___ ___ ___ ___!

Cloud Pictures

Round to the place of the underlined digit.

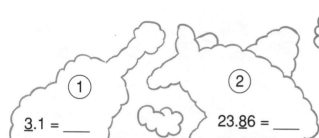

① 3.1 = ___

② 23.8_6 = ___

③ 4.9_08 = ___

④ 3.2_51 = ___

⑤ 1.0_7 = ___

⑥ 4._8 = ___

⑦ 2._547 = ___

⑧ 0.8_09 = ___

⑨ 0.6_09 = ___

⑩ 10._36 = ___

⑪ 0._98 = ___

⑫ 0.9_81 = ___

⑬ 1.9_08 = ___

⑭ 5._87 = ___

⑮ 6.05_9 = ___

Math Practice Pages • ©The Mailbox® Books • TEC61123 • Key p. 94

Gathering Clues

Add or subtract.

1.
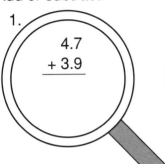
$$\begin{array}{r} 4.7 \\ + 3.9 \\ \hline \end{array}$$

2.

$$\begin{array}{r} 9.6 \\ - 2.8 \\ \hline \end{array}$$

3.
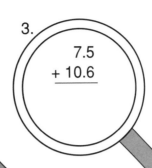
$$\begin{array}{r} 7.5 \\ + 10.6 \\ \hline \end{array}$$

4.

$$\begin{array}{r} 12.2 \\ - 6.3 \\ \hline \end{array}$$

5.
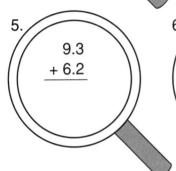
$$\begin{array}{r} 9.3 \\ + 6.2 \\ \hline \end{array}$$

6.
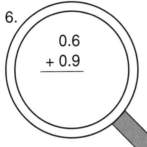
$$\begin{array}{r} 0.6 \\ + 0.9 \\ \hline \end{array}$$

7.

$$\begin{array}{r} 8.3 \\ - 3.7 \\ \hline \end{array}$$

8.

$$\begin{array}{r} 16.5 \\ - 10.9 \\ \hline \end{array}$$

9.

$$\begin{array}{r} 18 \\ - 6.9 \\ \hline \end{array}$$

10.

$$\begin{array}{r} 14.7 \\ - 10.7 \\ \hline \end{array}$$

11.
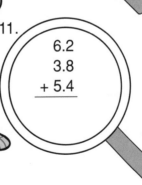
$$\begin{array}{r} 6.2 \\ 3.8 \\ + 5.4 \\ \hline \end{array}$$

12.
$$\begin{array}{r} 5.3 \\ 2.7 \\ + 4.1 \\ \hline \end{array}$$

Night at the Classroom

Add or subtract.

1. 5.78
    + 0.16
    Ⓗ

2. 0.57
    + 1.92
    Ⓔ

3. 5.46
    − 2.37
    Ⓞ

4. 11.97
    − 9.70
    Ⓞ

5. 1.73
    − 1.56
    Ⓨ

6. 8.01
    + 0.97
    Ⓖ

7. 15.76
    + 38.65
    Ⓞ

8. 0.29
    + 7.83
    Ⓛ

9. 11.06
    − 5.33
    Ⓣ

10. 25
    − 8.14
    Ⓜ

11. 7.38
    − 4.57
    Ⓢ

12. 18.06
    + 10.92
    Ⓔ

13. 7.05
    + 0.85
    Ⓡ

14. 3.82
    + 0.17
    Ⓦ

15. 6.27
    − 1.49
    Ⓔ

16. 0.72
    − 0.53
    Ⓐ

17. 6.56
    2.31
    + 0.45
    Ⓑ

18. 8
    − 3.21
    Ⓑ

19. 8.24
    − 3.65
    Ⓟ

20. 0.64
    5.92
    + 19.36
    Ⓥ

What did one math book say to the other?
To solve the riddle, write each letter from above
on its matching numbered line below.

___ ___ ___ ,   ___ ___ ___ ___   ___ ___
4.79 54.41 0.17   5.94 0.19 25.92 28.98   3.99 2.49

___ ___ ___   ___ ___ ___ ___ ___ ___ ___ !
8.98 3.09 5.73   4.59 7.9 2.27 9.32 8.12 4.78 16.86 2.81

Name _____   Date _____

Take a Look Inside

Add or subtract. Cross off each matching number
below. Two numbers will not be crossed off.

1. 12.64
    + 31.3
    _____

2. 9.5
    − 4.35
    _____

3. 58.2
    + 16.95
    _____

4. 609.37
    − 59.7
    _____

5. 43.02
    + 15
    _____

6. 273.86
    + 501.3
    _____

7. 825.4
    − 74.57
    _____

8. 183
    + 7.92
    _____

9. 913.79
    − 823.9
    _____

10. 36.65
     + 48.8
     _____

11. 540.5
     − 62.59
     _____

12. 11
     + 13.23
     _____

13. 72.7
     − 25.25
     _____

14. 38.9
     + 17.65
     _____

15. 963.81
     − 246.4
     _____

16. 14.33
     + 234.7
     _____

750.83	47.45	5.15
43.94	249.03	56.55
75.15	477.91	89.89
85.45	58.02	51.5
190.08	717.41	775.16
549.67	190.92	24.23

Name _____ Date _____

Something for a Sweet Tooth

Add or subtract.

1.
3.572
+ 2.838

2.
12.047
− 8.169

3.
0.669
+ 7.583

4.
5.725
− 0.925

5.
6.341
7.298
+ 0.706

6.
49.998
− 24.298

7.
63.566
2.013
+ 5.312

8.
37.214
− 19.845

9.
0.493
2.134
+ 7.893

10.
4.375
+ 3.927

11.
8.409
− 2.783

12.
0.534
+ 3.697

13.
36.391
1.049
+ 6.954

14.
6.315
− 0.893

15.
13.093
− 7.138

Name _____   Date _____

Tennis, Anyone?

Add or subtract. Write each answer in the grid.
The sum of each row and column should be 350.

1. 3.307
    + 5.08
    _____

2. 83.72
    + 2.4
    _____

3. 480
    − 258.354
    _____

4. 745
    − 711.153
    _____

5. 138.035
    + 10.43
    _____

6. 23.576
    − 7.428
    _____

7. 12.36
    + 23.947
    _____

8. 239.48
    − 90.4
    _____

9. 68.7
    + 3.08
    _____

10. 213.635
    − 21.39
    _____

11. 62.832
    − 24.131
    _____

12. 38.004
    + 9.27
    _____

13. 35.51 + 85.858 =

14. 46.337 + 9.15 =

15. 96.752 − 43.406 =

16. 224.599 − 104.8 =

Catching a Ride

Add or subtract.

1. $ 3.67
   + .15
   Ⓞ

2. $ 0.38
   + .85
   Ⓔ

3. $ 0.82
   − .65
   Ⓔ

4. $ 1.28
   .74
   + .12
   Ⓔ

5. $ 0.38
   .27
   + 19.85
   Ⓐ

6. $ 3.37
   − 1.28
   Ⓤ

7. $ 12.87
   − 8.50
   Ⓓ

8. $ 12.79
   + 48.62
   Ⓣ

9. $ 0.65
   − .37
   Ⓣ

10. $ 0.48
    .26
    + 18.95
    Ⓝ

11. $ 35.00
    − 21.95
    Ⓡ

12. $ 16.29
    − 11.85
    Ⓚ

13. $ 12.89
    − 7.80
    Ⓗ

14. $ 15.21
    − 13.75
    Ⓨ

15. $ 17.50
    − 6.51
    Ⓗ

16. $ 2.28
    .85
    + .17
    Ⓖ

What did one flea say to the other?

To solve the riddle, write each letter from above on its matching numbered line below.

Shall we walk home or

___ ___ ___ ___   ___ ___ ___   ___ ___ ___ ___ ___ ___ ___ ___ ___ ?
$61.41 $20.50 $4.44 $1.23 $0.28 $5.09 $0.17 $3.30 $13.05 $2.14 $1.46 $10.99 $3.82 $2.09 $19.69 $4.37

Name _____

Birds of a Feather

Estimate each sum or difference. Shade the feather with the matching answer.
Four answers will not be used.

54   202   9.24   2.23   53.08   57.03   15.13   13.12   78.18   55   11.75   203   49.0   56   14.14   10   8   49.9   25.4

Round to the nearest whole number.

A. 23.3
   + 32.2
   _____

B. 207.8
   −   5.4
   _____

C. 4.9
   + 2.6
   _____

Round to the nearest tenth.

D. 42.09
   + 6.85
   _____

E. 44.59
   + 5.33
   _____

F. 50.7
   − 25.25
   _____

Round to the nearest hundredth.

G. 17.436
   − 4.321
   _____

H. 7.532
   + 4.218
   _____

I. 75.426
   + 2.753
   _____

J. 48.804
   + 8.231
   _____

K. 59.456
   − 6.384
   _____

L. 22.567
   − 8.431
   _____

M. 4.678
   − 2.453
   _____

N. 17.436
   − 2.311
   _____

O. 12.456
   − 3.218
   _____

Math Practice Pages • ©The Mailbox® Books • TEC61123 • Key p. 95

Name _____   Date _____

Run the Race!

Solve.

1. Jill finished the race in 10.56 minutes. Austin finished the race 2.04 minutes after Jill. How long did it take Austin to run the race? _____

2. The winner of the race ran the course in 8.76 minutes. The person who finished last ran the race in 15.52 minutes. What is the difference between the first and last place times? _____

3. Last year the race course was 4.98 miles long. This year the course is 5.15 miles long. How much longer is the course this year than it was last year? _____

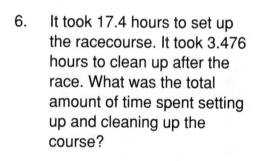

4. At the race, 71.83 percent of the runners wore sunglasses and 16.079 percent wore hats. What is the total percent of runners who wore sunglasses or hats? _____

6. It took 17.4 hours to set up the racecourse. It took 3.476 hours to clean up after the race. What was the total amount of time spent setting up and cleaning up the course?

_____

5. Jill's goal was to run the race in 12.24 minutes. She ran the race in 10.56 minutes. How much faster did she run the race than she had planned?

_____

Lazy River

Multiply. Shade your answer to show the path.

Start

#	Problem			
1.	0.7 x 4 =	2.8	0.28	28
2.	0.013 x 3 =	0.39	0.039	3.9
3.	1.376 x 5 =	68.80	6.880	688
4.	0.54 x 8 =	43.2	432	4.32
5.	0.9 x 7 =	0.63	63	6.3
6.	2.378 x 4 =	95.12	951.2	9.512
7.	6.01 x 9 =	5.409	54.09	540.9
8.	21.675 x 9 =	195.075	1,950.75	19,507.5
9.	8.09 x 6 =	48.54	4.854	4,854
10.	2.907 x 4 =	11.628	1,162.8	116.28
11.	0.016 x 5 =	8	0.080	0.8
12.	0.37 x 5 =	18.5	185	1.85
13.	0.012 x 5 =	6	0.060	0.6
14.	3.27 x 3 =	9.81	98.1	0.981
15.	3.025 x 9 =	27.225	272.25	2,722.5
16.	2.041 x 8 =	163.28	16.328	1,632.8

Finish

Name _____ Date _____

Question of the Day

Multiply.

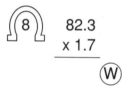 1) 5.6
    x 0.3
    (I)

2) 1.4
    x 0.5
    (N)

3) 27.5
    x 0.2
    (W)

4) 3.3
    x 0.8
    (N)

5) 45.8
    x 0.6
    (N)

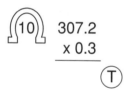 6) 124.3
    x 0.6
    (O)

7) 6.7
    x 3.8
    (S)

8) 82.3
    x 1.7
    (W)

9) 7.1
    x 4.9
    (T)

10) 307.2
    x 0.3
    (T)

11) 919.7
    x 0.6
    (H)

12) 54.5
    x 3.5
    (A)

13) 79.4
    x 6.7
    (Y)

When does a horse talk?
To solve the riddle, write each letter from above on its matching numbered line below.

" __ __ __ __ __ __ " __ __ __ __ __ __ __ __ !
139.91 551.82 1.68 2.64 0.70 531.98 5.50 190.75 27.48 92.16 25.46 34.79 74.58

Name _____ Date _____

Time For a Shake

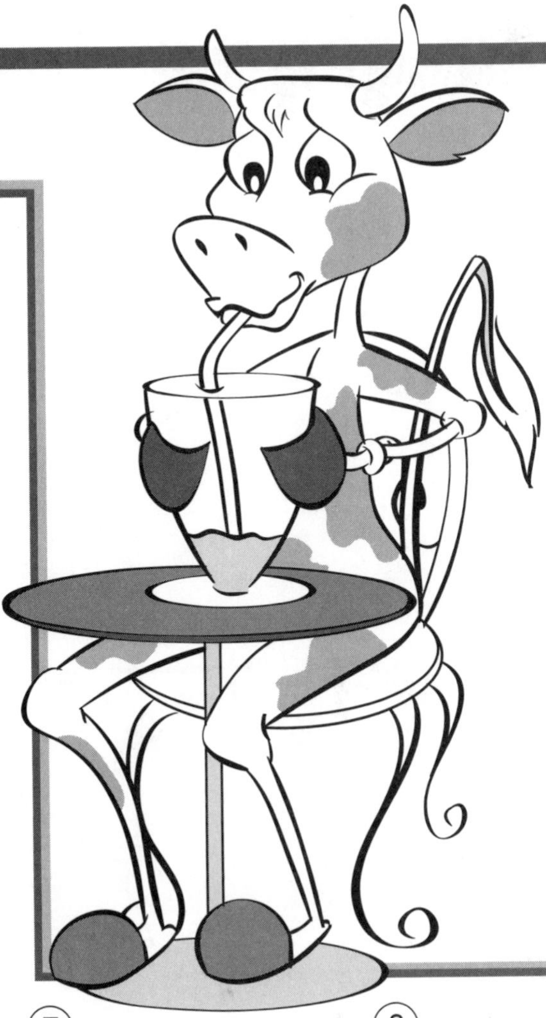

Multiply.

①
63.64
x 5.2
___

②
29.93
x 4.4
___

③
544.36
x 1.8
___

④
37.22
x 2.2
___

⑤
21.21
x 0.3
___

⑥
18.13
x 4.2
___

⑦
29.33
x 1.7
___

⑧
89.51
x 6.8
___

⑨
26.32
x 0.2
___

⑩
49.14
x 1.6
___

⑪
37.31
x 0.8
___

⑫
6.42
x 9.3
___

Hungry for Tacos

Multiply.

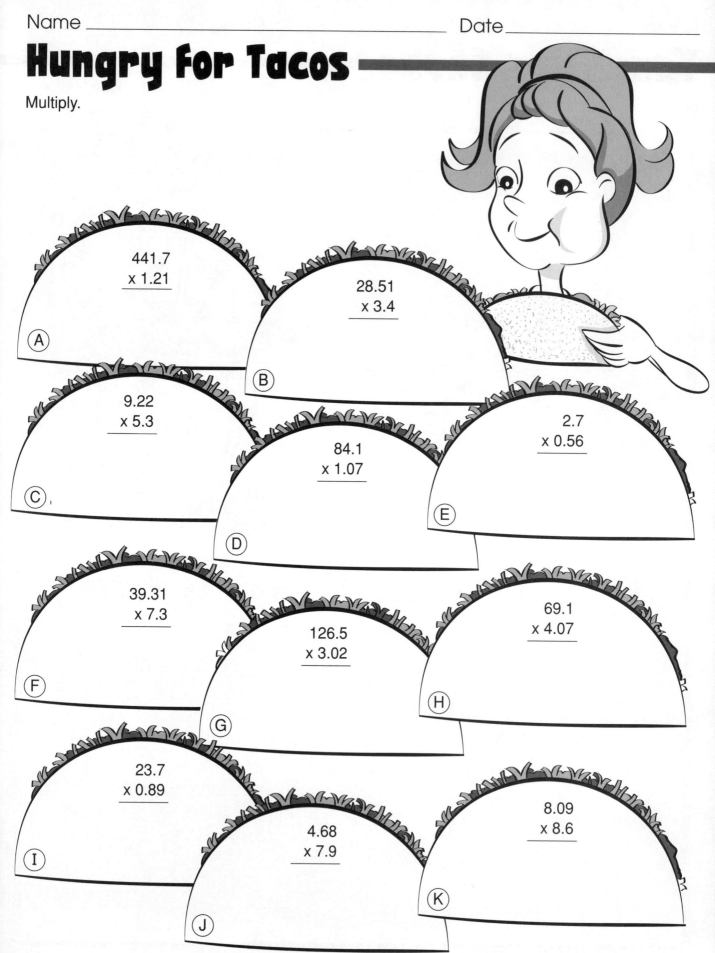

A. 441.7
    x 1.21

B. 28.51
    x 3.4

C. 9.22
    x 5.3

D. 84.1
    x 1.07

E. 2.7
    x 0.56

F. 39.31
    x 7.3

G. 126.5
    x 3.02

H. 69.1
    x 4.07

I. 23.7
    x 0.89

J. 4.68
    x 7.9

K. 8.09
    x 8.6

Name _____ Date _____

Beach Business

Solve.

1. Larry and Hermit sell items at the beach. A bottle of saltwater at their stand costs $1.15. If Larry and Hermit sell 12 bottles of saltwater, how much money will they make? _____

2. Hermit has three old shells he has outgrown. If he sells each shell for $6.24, how much money will he make? _____

3. Larry sells nine pretty seashells. If each shell weighs 8.7 ounces, how much do the seashells weigh in all? _____

4. Larry and Hermit have 10.5 pieces of seaweed for sale. Each piece is 10.81 inches long. How many inches of seaweed do they have for sale? _____

5. Larry sells eight bottles of sunscreen. If each bottle holds 7.25 ounces of sunscreen, how many ounces of sunscreen does he sell? _____

6. When business is slow, Larry and Hermit run laps around their stand. The distance around the stand is 16.5 feet. If they run around the stand 2.5 times, how far will they run? _____

Name _____ Date _____

Seating Problem

Divide. If the decimal part of the quotient is an even number, shade the box.

① $8\overline{)534.4}$	② $6\overline{)85.2}$	③ $4\overline{)56.4}$	④ $9\overline{)50.4}$
STAND	ASK	MISS	UP
⑤ $5\overline{)704.5}$	⑥ $2\overline{)389.4}$	⑦ $7\overline{)582.4}$	⑧ $3\overline{)124.8}$
MOST	OF	HIM	TO
⑨ $8\overline{)14.4}$	⑩ $4\overline{)89.2}$	⑪ $6\overline{)439.2}$	⑫ $2\overline{)895.4}$
PLEASE	THE	MOVE	MOVIE

What would you do if a hippo sat in front of you at the movies?
To solve the riddle, write the words from the unshaded boxes above in order on the lines below.

____ ____ ____ ____ ____

Hayride

Divide. Write your answer in the grid.
The sum of each row and column should be 100.

① 3⟌169.41

② 3⟌94.74

③ 6⟌71.70

④ 8⟌84.16

⑤ 6⟌70.86

⑥ 7⟌543.69

⑦ 9⟌297.09

⑧ 4⟌226.44

⑨ 5⟌51.90

Bessie's Been Busy

Divide.

1. $2 \overline{) 18.342}$

2. $4 \overline{) 649.916}$

3. $6 \overline{) 2.484}$

4. $8 \overline{) 75.416}$

5. $9 \overline{) 861.435}$

6. $7 \overline{) 34.041}$

7. $8 \overline{) 246.808}$

8. $3 \overline{) 45.678}$

9. $5 \overline{) 987.655}$

10. $6 \overline{) 495.744}$

Name _____ Date _____

Time for a Trim

Divide.

1. (T) $21\overline{)10.92}$

2. (T) $37\overline{)67.71}$

3. (H) $62\overline{)117.8}$

4. (O) $83\overline{)72.708}$

5. (S) $32\overline{)29.952}$

6. (S) $43\overline{)58.566}$

7. (C) $25\overline{)14.25}$

8. (R) $58\overline{)3,387.2}$

9. (U) $32\overline{)13.12}$

Why do barbers make good drivers?
To solve the riddle, write each letter from above on its matching numbered line below.

Because they know all the ___ ___ ___ ___ ___   ___ ___ ___ ___!
1.362 1.9 0.876 58.4 0.52   0.57 0.41 1.83 0.936

Birds, Baths, and "Bee-yond"

Solve.

1. Bonnie Bee sells five birdbaths to Jay Bird. If he pays Bonnie a total of $125.25, how much does each birdbath cost?

   _____

2. Ella Yellow Jacket buys 12 packs of sunflower seeds from Bonnie. If Ella pays Bonnie $14.76, how much does each pack of seeds cost?

   _____

3. Bonnie Bee is ordering more flowerpots. The bill is $539.66. If she is buying 22 flowerpots, how much does each pot cost?

   _____

4. On Saturday and Sunday, Bonnie sold a total of 864.34 pounds of mulch for flower beds. If she sold the same amount of mulch each day, how many pounds did she sell on Saturday?

   _____

5. Randy Robin is buying statues for his garden. The statues weigh a total of 175.176 pounds. If he buys eight statues, how much does each statue weigh?

   _____

6. After working for seven days, Bonnie made $4,999.47 from her business. If she made the same amount of money each day, how much did she make on Wednesday?

   _____

Answer Keys

Page 4
1. 10,000 + 5,000 + 600 + 40 + 1
2. 814,211
3. eight hundred forty-one thousand, two hundred one
4. 5,640; 5,000 + 600 + 40
5. one million, four hundred thousand, two hundred two; 1,000,000 + 400,000 + 200 + 2

Page 5
1. incorrect
2. correct
3. incorrect
4. incorrect
5. correct
6. incorrect
7. correct
8. incorrect
9. correct
10. correct
11. incorrect
12. correct
13. incorrect
14. correct
15. incorrect
16. incorrect
17. correct
18. correct

The crook was caught at the corner
OF ELM STREET AND VINE.

Page 6
1. ten = 1,887,650
   hundred = 1,887,700
   thousand = 1,888,000
   ten thousand = 1,890,000
   hundred thousand = 1,900,000
   million = 2,000,000

2. ten = 3,406,790
   hundred = 3,406,800
   thousand = 3,407,000
   ten thousand = 3,410,000
   hundred thousand = 3,400,000
   million = 3,000,000

3. ten = 5,056,140
   hundred = 5,056,100
   thousand = 5,056,000
   ten thousand = 5,060,000
   hundred thousand = 5,100,000
   million = 5,000,000

4. ten = 8,107,450
   hundred = 8,107,500
   thousand = 8,107,000
   ten thousand = 8,110,000
   hundred thousand = 8,100,000
   million = 8,000,000

5. ten = 4,610,050
   hundred = 4,610,000
   thousand = 4,610,000
   ten thousand = 4,610,000
   hundred thousand = 4,600,000
   million = 5,000,000

6. ten = 2,864,210
   hundred = 2,864,200
   thousand = 2,864,000
   ten thousand = 2,860,000
   hundred thousand = 2,900,000
   million = 3,000,000

Page 7
1. <
2. >
3. <
4. >
5. >
6. <
7. <
8. <
9. >
10. <
11. 301; 3,001; 3,010; 3,100; 3,030,001
12. 1,011; 1,101; 10,001; 10,010; 10,011
13. 325; 906; 2,358; 2,620
14. 286; 590; 5,590; 18,137
15. 679; 6,738; 660,984; 662,720

Page 8
1. 643
2. 1,607
3. 980
4. 52,936
5. 4,080
6. 1,844
7. 10,658
8. 1,000
9. 609
10. 1,199
11. 5,500
12. 21,100

Page 9
1. 1,975
2. 9,999
3. 744,480
4. 10,700
5. 53,037
6. 2,505
7. 10,000
8. 9,434
9. 11,891
10. 364,690

an ACCOUNTANT

Page 10
1. 1,774
2. 2,779
3. 189
4. 56,033
5. 3,875
6. 75,291
7. 2,689
8. 187,065
9. 2,236
10. 488,868

Page 11
1. 1,065
2. 1,356
3. 2,108
4. 23,882
5. 709
6. 9,199
7. 31,670
8. $983.72

Page 12
1. C
2. B
3. A
4. B
5. D
6. A
7. C
8. A
9. D
10. C

Page 13
1. 21
2. 32
3. 24
4. 24
5. 49
6. 28
7. 64
8. 54
9. 42
10. 63
11. 81
12. 56
13. 27
14. 48
15. 72
16. 48
17. 24
18. 0
19. 30
20. 63

Page 14
1. 4,200
2. 4,500
3. 3,500
4. 3,200
5. $27.00
6. 1,800
7. 2,400
8. 4,000
9. $72.00
10. 25,000
11. 16,000
12. $120.00
13. 49,000
14. 48,000
15. 63,000

A COLD-CUT SPECIAL

Page 15
1. 1,500
2. 1,200
3. 4,000
4. 2,000
5. 800
6. 3,000
7. 3,600
8. 2,100
9. 1,800
10. 8,000
11. 5,600
12. 3,200

The code is <u>6-2-0-0</u>.

Page 16
1. R: 80,000; F-E: 60,000
2. R: 280,000; F-E: 240,000
3. R: 160,000; F-E: 160,000
4. R: 400,000; F-E: 350,000
5. R: 180,000; F-E: 160,000
6. R: 240,000; F-E: 180,000

Page 17
1. 120,000
2. 150,000
3. 20,000
4. 240,000
5. 160,000
6. 40,000
7. 60,000
8. $90,000

Page 18

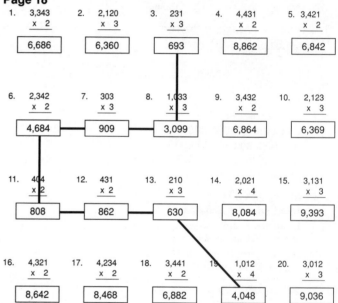

Page 19
1. 714
2. 168
3. 492
4. 840
5. 319
6. 407
7. 713
8. 169
9. 2,387
10. 1,694
11. 6,680
12. 2,688
13. 5,709
14. 9,526
15. 96,657
16. 107,943
17. 91,161
18. 28,224
19. 39,403
20. 71,829

SIR GAWAIN and SIR BEDIVERE

Page 20
1. 91,908
2. 420,024
3. 30,492
4. 763,830
5. 29,768
6. 729,603
7. 65,246
8. 906,984
9. 97,656
10. 174,361

Page 21
1. 9,546
2. 14,985
3. 15,708
4. 47,531
5. 409,464

Page 22
1. 98
2. 966
3. 136
4. 5,560
5. 763
6. 8,052
7. 1,026
8. 10,266
9. 908
10. 8,964

A PORCUPINE

Page 23
1. 325
2. 41,364
3. 5,916
4. 364
5. 8,920
6. 377
7. 37,481
8. 7,452
9. 240
10. 70,119

COME BACK

Page 24
1. 24,852
2. 307,521
3. 368,606
4. 41,552
5. 25,521
6. 196,080
7. 410,674
8. 38,252
9. 55,902
10. 502,208

Page 25
1. 455
2. 1,740
3. 3,136
4. 4,896
5. 28,182

Page 26
1. 1,428
2. 4,858
3. 4,932
4. 2,268
5. 4,914
6. 3,012
7. 17,030
8. 48,601
9. 15,136
10. 38,367
11. 52,808
12. 76,584

Page 27
1. 7,050
2. 1,247
3. 2,808
4. 1,392
5. 17,784
6. 9,471
7. 44,528
8. 304,308
9. 248,160
10. 297,927

Page 28
1. 185,886
2. 1,778,772
3. 726,264
4. 2,528,395
5. 192,794
6. 1,282,659
7. 483,072
8. 816,075

The final bid was $4,817,885.00.

Page 29
1. 768
2. 91,292
3. 814
4. 97,104
5. 306,375

Page 30

54 ÷ 9 = 6 (1)	63 ÷ 7 = 9 (2)	28 ÷ 4 = 7 (3)

18 ÷ 6 = 3 (4)	24 ÷ 6 = 4 (5)	20 ÷ 5 = 4 (6)	32 ÷ 8 = 4 (7)	42 ÷ 7 = 6 (8)
35 ÷ 7 = 5 (9)	36 ÷ 9 = 4 (10)	40 ÷ 8 = 5 (11)	21 ÷ 7 = 3 (12)	32 ÷ 4 = 8 (13)
24 ÷ 3 = 8 (14)	27 ÷ 3 = 9 (15)	48 ÷ 6 = 8 (16)	36 ÷ 4 = 9 (17)	45 ÷ 5 = 9 (18)
49 ÷ 7 = 7 (19)	30 ÷ 6 = 5 (20)	14 ÷ 7 = 2 (21)	12 ÷ 4 = 3 (22)	18 ÷ 9 = 2 (23)

64 ÷ 8 = 8 (24)

Page 31
A. 20
200
2,000
20,000

B. 90
900
9,000
90,000

C. 90
900
9,000
90,000

D. 60
600
6,000
60,000

E. 60
600
6,000
60,000

F. 80
800
8,000
80,000

G. 3
30
300
3,000

H. 7
70
700
7,000

Page 32
1. 400
2. 50
3. 60
4. 40
5. 90
6. 90
7. 70
8. 300
9. 60
10. 100
11. 20
12. 80

PICK ON SOMEONE YOUR OWN SIZE!

Page 33
A. 200
B. 800
C. 900
D. 700
E. 200
F. 800
G. 300
H. 400
I. 500
J. 600
K. 100
L. 300
Quotients from 100 to 400: A, E, G, H, K, L
Quotients from 500 to 900: B, C, D, F, I, J

Page 34
A. 13
B. 46
C. 12
D. 18
E. 26
F. 161
G. 120
H. 101
I. 121
J. 342
K. 1,570
L. 1,563
M. 2,198
N. 2,124
O. 1,412

Page 35
1. 4 R2
2. 15 R3
3. 59 R6
4. 59 R8
5. 528 R1
6. 723 R2
7. 25 R1
8. 12 R4
9. 82 R3
10. 963 R6
11. 13 R5
12. 11 R7
13. 76 R5
14. 239 R3

BY THE "HARES" IN IT!

Page 36
1. 23 days
2. 15 omelets
3. 77 chocolate chips
4. 16 calories
5. 109 cereals
6. 149 pieces

Page 37
1. 9 hangers
2. 10 loads
3. 32 trips
4. 51 weeks
5. 629 clotheslines
6. 818 bags

Page 38
1. 50
2. 12
3. 4
4. 2
5. 52
6. 66
7. 56
8. 6
9. 62
10. 60
11. 38
12. 23
13. 700
14. 1,232
15. 211

Page 39
1. 7 R2
2. 11 R7
3. 8 R5
4. 11 R4
5. 6 R16
6. 2 R10
7. 12 R3
8. 5 R11
9. 6 R12
10. 5 R13
11. 63 R1
12. 26 R14
13. 64 R9
14. 63 R8
15. 67 R15
16. 5,173 R6

5 16	7 3	1 2	10 13
3 5	6 10	8 11	14 8
13 9	16 6	2 7	9 12
4 4	15 15	12 14	11 1

Page 40
1. 4 R18
2. 2 R28
3. 11 R7
4. 3 R28
5. 212 R3
6. 132 R1
7. 147 R13
8. 56 R4
9. 566 R13
10. 1,631 R26
11. 355 R25
12. 751 R25

Page 41
1. 30 R5
2. 10 R26
3. 20 R15
4. 30 R11
5. 50 R12
6. 200 R20
7. 302 R2
8. 304 R36
9. 401 R10
10. 760 R29

Page 42

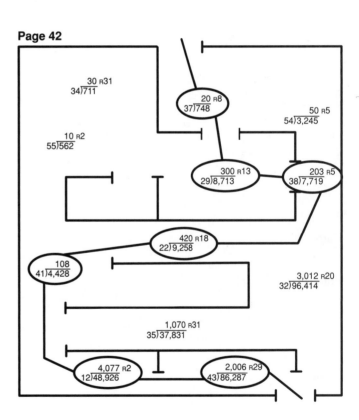

Page 43
1. 9 crates
2. 120 acres
3. 84 pounds
4. 175 tomatoes
5. 2,059 baskets
6. 3,093 cartons

Page 44

A. $\frac{1}{6}$, $\frac{5}{30}$ B. $\frac{9}{15}$, $\frac{3}{5}$ C. $\frac{6}{8}$, $\frac{3}{4}$ D. $\frac{2}{8}$, $\frac{1}{4}$

E. $\frac{2}{10}$, $\frac{1}{5}$ F. $\frac{6}{21}$, $\frac{4}{14}$ G. $\frac{4}{6}$, $\frac{6}{9}$ H. $\frac{2}{9}$, $\frac{6}{27}$

I. $\frac{9}{30}$, $\frac{3}{10}$ J. $\frac{8}{12}$, $\frac{2}{3}$ K. $\frac{10}{25}$, $\frac{2}{5}$ L. $\frac{24}{32}$, $\frac{3}{4}$

Page 45

1. $\frac{5}{8}$ 9. $\frac{1}{4}$

2. $\frac{2}{5}$ 10. $\frac{3}{6}$

3. $\frac{4}{15}$ 11. $\frac{1}{2}$

4. $\frac{7}{9}$ 12. $\frac{4}{9}$

5. $\frac{4}{9}$ 13. $\frac{17}{20}$

6. $\frac{9}{10}$ 14. $\frac{4}{5}$

7. $\frac{5}{14}$ 15. $\frac{5}{20}$

8. $\frac{7}{16}$ 16. $\frac{7}{8}$

SWALLOW THE LEADER

Page 46

A. $\frac{1}{2}$ B. $\frac{1}{3}$ C. $\frac{2}{3}$ D. $\frac{1}{5}$

E. $\frac{3}{4}$ F. $\frac{1}{3}$ G. $\frac{1}{4}$ H. $\frac{1}{2}$ I. $\frac{5}{7}$

J. $\frac{3}{4}$ K. $\frac{3}{4}$ L. $\frac{1}{3}$ M. $\frac{2}{3}$

N. $\frac{4}{5}$ O. $\frac{1}{4}$ P. $\frac{1}{2}$ Q. $\frac{1}{5}$

R. $\frac{1}{8}$

Page 47

Fractions in a circle: $\frac{1}{5}$, $\frac{2}{13}$, $\frac{1}{6}$, $\frac{1}{8}$, $\frac{3}{20}$, $\frac{1}{7}$

Fractions in a triangle: $\frac{4}{7}$, $\frac{5}{8}$, $\frac{7}{12}$, $\frac{8}{15}$, $\frac{9}{20}$, $\frac{6}{11}$

Fractions in a box: $\frac{18}{21}$, $\frac{4}{5}$, $\frac{7}{8}$, $\frac{5}{6}$, $\frac{9}{10}$, $\frac{8}{9}$, $\frac{11}{12}$, $\frac{14}{15}$, $\frac{24}{25}$

Page 48

1. $\frac{1}{2}$ 2. $1\frac{3}{4}$ 3. $\frac{2}{5}$ 4. $\frac{1}{2}$

5. $1\frac{1}{5}$ 6. $\frac{2}{3}$ 7. $\frac{1}{2}$ 8. $1\frac{1}{2}$

9. $\frac{2}{3}$ 10. $\frac{1}{4}$ 11. $\frac{1}{5}$ 12. $\frac{4}{5}$

13. $1\frac{5}{9}$ 14. 2 15. $\frac{3}{8}$ 16. $1\frac{1}{2}$

17. $\frac{2}{3}$ 18. $\frac{13}{14}$ 19. $\frac{1}{8}$ 20. $\frac{2}{3}$

21. $\frac{1}{2}$ 22. $\frac{1}{4}$ 23. $1\frac{1}{4}$ 24. $\frac{1}{4}$

Page 49

1. $1\frac{1}{8}$

2. $\frac{7}{24}$

3. $1\frac{1}{6}$

4. $2\frac{1}{8}$

5. $\frac{3}{20}$

6. $\frac{1}{18}$

7. $1\frac{1}{4}$

8. $1\frac{1}{2}$

9. $\frac{7}{8}$

10. $\frac{1}{15}$

11. $\frac{2}{3}$

12. $1\frac{3}{8}$

<u>6</u> towels

Page 50

1. $\frac{6}{7}$ of the messages

2. $\frac{1}{4}$ more time

3. $\frac{14}{15}$ of the points

4. Alex needs $\frac{2}{5}$ of the money. Jay needs $\frac{4}{5}$ of the money.

5. $\frac{4}{5}$ of the computers

6. $\frac{2}{3}$ longer

Page 51

1. $\frac{3}{4}$ of the pies

2. $\frac{13}{24}$ of the pie

3. $\frac{33}{40}$ of the pie

4. $\frac{1}{24}$ more peach pie

5. $\frac{1}{12}$ inch thicker

6. $\frac{5}{6}$ of the pies

Page 52

1. $4\frac{3}{4}$

2. $10\frac{1}{2}$

3. $4\frac{2}{3}$

4. $2\frac{1}{5}$

5. $6\frac{1}{3}$

6. $5\frac{1}{3}$

7. $9\frac{2}{5}$

8. $1\frac{3}{4}$

9. $2\frac{1}{3}$

10. $3\frac{1}{2}$

11. $7\frac{7}{8}$

12. $9\frac{4}{5}$

"TWEETMENT"!

Page 53

1. $7\frac{8}{15}$
2. $2\frac{1}{4}$
3. $9\frac{5}{9}$
4. $7\frac{1}{3}$
5. $9\frac{1}{8}$
6. $2\frac{1}{3}$
7. $9\frac{1}{4}$
8. $3\frac{1}{2}$
9. $13\frac{1}{9}$
10. $6\frac{5}{8}$

Page 54

1. $10\frac{1}{4}$ 2. $8\frac{3}{10}$ 3. $4\frac{1}{8}$
4. $5\frac{7}{10}$ 5. $11\frac{1}{4}$ 6. $12\frac{11}{24}$
7. $\frac{7}{9}$ 8. $3\frac{3}{16}$ 9. $6\frac{3}{4}$
10. $10\frac{1}{2}$ 11. $7\frac{1}{2}$ 12. $\frac{1}{3}$

Page 55

1. $6\frac{1}{2}$ shelves
2. 3 cups
3. $5\frac{8}{9}$ hours
4. $12\frac{3}{4}$ boxes
5. $3\frac{1}{4}$ cups
6. $5\frac{1}{5}$ feet

Page 56

1. $5\frac{7}{40}$ scoops
2. $2\frac{2}{21}$ waffle cones
3. $5\frac{5}{12}$ shelves
4. $5\frac{1}{6}$ hours
5. $3\frac{1}{2}$ cartons
6. $22\frac{1}{12}$ boxes

Page 57

1. $\frac{1}{4}$ 2. $\frac{7}{15}$
3. $\frac{6}{35}$ 4. $\frac{1}{18}$
5. $\frac{2}{15}$ 6. $\frac{35}{54}$
7. $\frac{3}{8}$ 8. $\frac{1}{10}$
9. $\frac{1}{6}$ 10. $\frac{3}{32}$
11. $\frac{15}{56}$ 12. $\frac{2}{21}$

There <u>once</u> was a young <u>man</u> from <u>France</u>
Who <u>tore</u> a big <u>hole</u> in his <u>pants</u>.
He <u>bought</u> a new <u>pair</u>,
So he'd have <u>something</u> to <u>wear</u>
When he went with his <u>friends</u> to a <u>dance</u>.

Page 58

1. $\frac{5}{18}$ 2. $\frac{2}{5}$
3. $\frac{1}{6}$ 4. $\frac{5}{8}$
5. $\frac{1}{20}$ 6. $\frac{1}{6}$
7. $\frac{9}{25}$ 8. $\frac{7}{16}$
9. $\frac{3}{32}$ 10. $\frac{5}{12}$

"<u>COMEDI-HENS</u>"!

Page 59

1. $\frac{2}{9}$ 2. $\frac{2}{3}$ 3. $\frac{1}{10}$ 4. $\frac{4}{35}$ 5. $\frac{1}{15}$
6. $\frac{1}{10}$ 7. $\frac{5}{9}$ 8. $\frac{1}{10}$ 9. $\frac{5}{14}$
10. $\frac{1}{2}$ 11. $\frac{3}{20}$ 12. $\frac{1}{6}$
13. $\frac{7}{18}$ 14. $\frac{3}{5}$

Page 60

1. $1\frac{2}{5}$
2. $2\frac{1}{4}$
3. $4\frac{1}{2}$
4. 2
5. $2\frac{2}{3}$
6. 3
7. $1\frac{5}{7}$
8. $1\frac{7}{8}$
9. $1\frac{3}{4}$
10. $5\frac{3}{5}$
11. $1\frac{2}{3}$
12. $1\frac{7}{9}$
13. $2\frac{7}{10}$
14. $\frac{1}{4}$
15. $\frac{1}{2}$

Page 61

1.	3	7.	5	13.	$4\frac{4}{5}$
2.	$2\frac{1}{2}$	8.	$\frac{1}{3}$	14.	$\frac{1}{4}$
3.	$1\frac{3}{4}$	9.	4	15.	$1\frac{7}{9}$
4.	$2\frac{4}{5}$	10.	$3\frac{1}{2}$	16.	$\frac{1}{2}$
5.	$1\frac{7}{8}$	11.	$3\frac{3}{7}$	17.	10
6.	$1\frac{1}{5}$	12.	$2\frac{2}{5}$	18.	6

Page 62

1.	$\frac{5}{8}$	8.	$1\frac{1}{7}$
2.	$1\frac{2}{3}$	9.	$\frac{9}{10}$
3.	$\frac{13}{16}$	10.	$\frac{2}{5}$
4.	$\frac{7}{12}$	11.	$\frac{3}{10}$
5.	$1\frac{7}{10}$	12.	$1\frac{5}{8}$
6.	$\frac{23}{42}$	13.	$1\frac{5}{8}$
7.	$1\frac{9}{40}$	14.	$\frac{1}{2}$

Page 63

1.	20	6.	$3\frac{1}{4}$	11.	$7\frac{1}{3}$
2.	$2\frac{2}{3}$	7.	$2\frac{5}{6}$	12.	26
3.	3	8.	2	13.	6
4.	$3\frac{8}{9}$	9.	9	14.	$4\frac{1}{2}$
5.	$7\frac{1}{2}$	10.	$6\frac{8}{9}$	15.	$8\frac{1}{4}$

Page 64

1. $\frac{1}{10}$ of the money
2. $1\frac{3}{10}$ of the bags
3. $\frac{1}{5}$ of their money
4. $\frac{1}{4}$ of the shoppers
5. 10 of the clothing stores
6. $4\frac{1}{8}$ hours

Page 65

1. 0.07
2. 2.3
3. 0.715
4. 0.6
5. 3.06
6. 0.008
7. sixty-seven and ninety-eight hundredths
8. one and eight tenths
9. seven thousandths
10. one and three hundred seventy-five thousandths
11. one and two tenths
12. five and two hundredths
13. 2 tenths
14. 5 hundredths
15. 7 tenths
16. 3 hundredths
17. 4 thousandths
18. 3 tenths
19. 7 hundredths
20. 6 thousandths
21. 5 hundredths
22. 5 thousandths
23. 1 tenth
24. 2 thousandths

Page 66

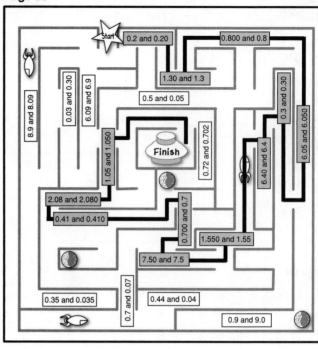

Page 67

①	4.4 < 4.04	Ⓓ 8.2 < 8.15	Ⓒ 0.11 < 0.29	Ⓘ
②	0.86 < 0.68	Ⓑ 39.42 < 39.4	Ⓐ 4.5 < 5.4	Ⓣ
③	8.06 < 8.03	Ⓔ 3.15 > 3.015	Ⓢ 3.4 < 3.3	Ⓤ
④	10.64 < 10.63	Ⓕ 10.50 < 10.75	Ⓒ 0.13 < 0.10	Ⓖ
⑤	7.015 < 7.105	Ⓡ 20.02 < 20.01	Ⓘ 9.65 < 9.26	Ⓗ
⑥	5.16 < 5.06	Ⓚ 9.56 < 9.86	Ⓔ 14.17 > 14.2	Ⓛ
⑦	29.71 > 29.713	Ⓝ 80.6 < 81.6	Ⓜ 4.25 > 4.025	Ⓓ
⑧	7.21 > 7.225	Ⓞ 1.3 < 2.7	Ⓘ 60.6 < 6.06	Ⓟ
⑨	6.013 < 6.310	Ⓣ 0.14 > 0.15	Ⓢ 0.98 < 0.908	Ⓡ
⑩	8.023 > 8.005	Ⓒ 33.1 > 33.11	Ⓦ 2.31 > 6.5	Ⓐ
⑪	45.07 > 45.57	Ⓒ 0.2 > 0.19	Ⓐ 5.2 < 5.17	Ⓑ
⑫	23.0 > 32.0	Ⓓ 17.02 < 18.20	Ⓡ 13.94 > 13.95	Ⓕ
⑬	6.53 < 6.5	Ⓗ 0.21 > 0.27	Ⓖ 14.25 < 14.38	Ⓓ
⑭	0.08 > 8.0	Ⓔ 5.40 > 5.41	Ⓚ 80.6 > 8.06	Ⓢ

TAKE AWAY <u>ITS CREDIT CARDS</u>!

Page 68

1.	3	2.	23.9	3.	4.91	4.	3.25
5.	1.1	6.	5	7.	2.5	8.	0.8
9.	0.61	10.	10	11.	1	12.	1.0
13.	1.91	14.	5.9	15.	6.06		

Page 69

1.	8.6	7.	4.6
2.	6.8	8.	5.6
3.	18.1	9.	11.1
4.	5.9	10.	4
5.	15.5	11.	15.4
6.	1.5	12.	12.1

Page 70

1.	5.94	11.	2.81
2.	2.49	12.	28.98
3.	3.09	13.	7.9
4.	2.27	14.	3.99
5.	0.17	15.	4.78
6.	8.98	16.	0.19
7.	54.41	17.	9.32
8.	8.12	18.	4.79
9.	5.73	19.	4.59
10.	16.86	20.	25.92

BOY, HAVE WE GOT PROBLEMS!

Page 71

1.	43.94	9.	89.89
2.	5.15	10.	85.45
3.	75.15	11.	477.91
4.	549.67	12.	24.23
5.	58.02	13.	47.45
6.	775.16	14.	56.55
7.	750.83	15.	717.41
8.	190.92	16.	249.03

Page 72

1.	6.410	9.	10.52
2.	3.878	10.	8.302
3.	8.252	11.	5.626
4.	4.8	12.	4.231
5.	14.345	13.	44.394
6.	25.7	14.	5.422
7.	70.891	15.	5.955
8.	17.369		

Page 73

1.	8.387	9.	71.78
2.	86.12	10.	192.245
3.	221.646	11.	38.701
4.	33.847	12.	47.274
5.	148.465	13.	121.368
6.	16.148	14.	55.487
7.	36.307	15.	53.346
8.	149.08	16.	119.799

① 8.387	② 86.12	③ 221.646	④ 33.847
⑤ 148.465	⑥ 16.148	⑦ 36.307	⑧ 149.08
⑨ 71.78	⑩ 192.245	⑪ 38.701	⑫ 47.274
⑬ 121.368	⑭ 55.487	⑮ 53.346	⑯ 119.799

Page 74

1.	$3.82	9.	$0.28
2.	$1.23	10.	$19.69
3.	$0.17	11.	$13.05
4.	$2.14	12.	$4.44
5.	$20.50	13.	$5.09
6.	$2.09	14.	$1.46
7.	$4.37	15.	$10.99
8.	$61.41	16.	$3.30

Shall we walk home or TAKE THE GREYHOUND?

Page 75

A. 55
B. 203
C. 8
D. 49.0
E. 49.9
F. 25.4
G. 13.12
H. 11.75
I. 78.18
J. 57.03
K. 53.08
L. 14.14
M. 2.23
N. 15.13
O. 9.24

Page 76

1. 12.60 minutes
2. 6.76 minutes
3. 0.17 mile
4. 87.909 percent
5. 1.68 minutes
6. 20.876 hours

Page 77

1. 0.7 x 4 = 2.8	**2.8**	0.28	28
2. 0.013 x 3 = 0.039	0.39	**0.039**	3.9
3. 1.376 x 5 = 6.880	68.80	**6.880**	688
4. 0.54 x 8 = 4.32	43.2	432	**4.32**
5. 0.9 x 7 = 6.3	0.63	63	**6.3**
6. 2.378 x 4 = 9.512	95.12	951.2	**9.512**
7. 6.01 x 9 = 54.09	5.409	**54.09**	540.9
8. 21.675 x 9 = 195.075	**195.075**	1,950.75	19,507.5
9. 8.09 x 6 = 48.54	**48.54**	4.854	4,854
10. 2.907 x 4 = 11.628	**11.628**	1,162.8	116.28
11. 0.016 x 5 = 0.080	8	**0.080**	0.8
12. 0.37 x 5 = 1.85	18.5	185	**1.85**
13. 0.012 x 5 = 0.060	6	**0.060**	0.6
14. 3.27 x 3 = 9.81	**9.81**	98.1	0.981
15. 3.025 x 9 = 27.225	**27.225**	272.25	2,722.5
16. 2.041 x 8 = 16.328	163.28	**16.328**	1,632.8

Page 78
1. 1.68
2. 0.70
3. 5.50
4. 2.64
5. 27.48
6. 74.58
7. 25.46
8. 139.91
9. 34.79
10. 92.16
11. 551.82
12. 190.75
13. 531.98

"WHINNY" WANTS TO!

Page 79
1. 330.928
2. 131.692
3. 979.848
4. 81.884
5. 6.363
6. 76.146
7. 49.861
8. 608.668
9. 5.264
10. 78.624
11. 29.848
12. 59.706

Page 80
A. 534.457
B. 96.934
C. 48.866
D. 89.987
E. 1.512
F. 286.963
G. 382.030
H. 281.237
I. 21.093
J. 36.972
K. 69.574

Page 81
1. $13.80
2. $18.72
3. 78.3 ounces
4. 113.505 inches
5. 58 ounces
6. 41.25 feet

Page 82

① 66.8 8)534.4 STAND	② 14.2 6)85.2 ASK	③ 14.1 4)56.4 MISS	④ 5.6 9)50.4 UP
⑤ 140.9 5)704.5 MOST	⑥ 194.7 2)389.4 OF	⑦ 83.2 7)582.4 HIM	⑧ 41.6 3)124.8 TO
⑨ 1.8 8)14.4 PLEASE	⑩ 22.3 4)89.2 THE	⑪ 73.2 6)439.2 MOVE	⑫ 447.7 2)895.4 MOVIE

MISS MOST OF THE MOVIE

Page 83
1. 56.47
2. 31.58
3. 11.95
4. 10.52
5. 11.81
6. 77.67
7. 33.01
8. 56.61
9. 10.38

① 56.47	② 31.58	③ 11.95
④ 10.52	⑤ 11.81	⑥ 77.67
⑦ 33.01	⑧ 56.61	⑨ 10.38

Page 84
1. 9.171
2. 162.479
3. 0.414
4. 9.427
5. 95.715
6. 4.863
7. 30.851
8. 15.226
9. 197.531
10. 82.624

Page 85
1. 0.52
2. 1.83
3. 1.9
4. 0.876
5. 0.936
6. 1.362
7. 0.57
8. 58.4
9. 0.41

Because they know all the SHORT CUTS!

Page 86
1. $25.05
2. $1.23
3. $24.53
4. 432.17 pounds
5. 21.897 pounds
6. $714.21